IMAGES
of America

THE PORTUGUESE
IN SAN LEANDRO

ON THE COVER: UPEC OFFICERS IN FRONT OF CITY HALL ON DAVIS STREET, 1888. Pictured from left to right are Carl Iversen, Joseph Bettencourt, Manuel Andrade, Manuel Rodgers, Jesse Woods, Joseph Olympia, Manuel Braga, Joe Barbara, and Manuel Avilla. (*Portuguese Immigrants.*)

IMAGES
of America

THE PORTUGUESE
IN SAN LEANDRO

Meg Rogers with
the support of the J. A. Freitas Library

ARCADIA
PUBLISHING

Published by Arcadia Publishing
Charleston, South Carolina

Library of Congress Catalog Card Number: 2007943435

For all general information contact Arcadia Publishing at:
Telephone 843-853-2070
Fax 843-853-0044
E-mail sales@arcadiapublishing.com
For customer service and orders:
Toll-Free 1-888-313-2665

Visit us on the Internet at www.arcadiapublishing.com

"*Forty years ago old Silva came from the Azores. Went sheep-herdin' in the mountains a couple of years, then blew into San Leandro. These five acres was the first land he leased. That was the beginnin'. Then he began leasin' by the hundreds of acres, an' by the hundred-an sixties. An' his sisters an' his uncles an' his aunts begun pouring' in from the Azores—they're all related there, you know; an' pretty soon San Leandro was a regular Porchugeeze settlement.*" —Jack London, Valley of the Moon, 1913.

MANUEL ANDRADE, WHALER. In 1859, Andrade worked on a whaling vessel off the coast of Hawaii before immigrating to San Leandro. Leaving his native island of Faial for Flores, Andrade signed a contract to hunt whales aboard the *Bark Pacific*. For two years, Andrade tracked the mammals around the Horn, in Russia's OKOTSK Sea, and off the Hawaiian coast, a job that Andrade describes as an "amphibious factory." Andrade's journal describes the day in Honolulu when he quit his job: "Paying a man to go in my place in accordance with the law of the United States, since I had been contracted for the remainder of the voyage. On November 7, and from shore, I waved good-bye to the 'Pacific' when she left for home after a whale hunting trip which netted 52 whales, 3,700 barrels of oil and 24,000 pounds of bones." Many Portuguese immigrants came to California as shore whalers. Later they came to pan for gold. Once in California, they found California's real gold—a fertile soil that would feed the nation. (*Portuguese Immigrants*.)

CONTENTS

ACKNOWLEDGMENTS

While writing Arcadia's Images of America: *The Portuguese in San Jose*, I found numerous references to the Portuguese community of San Leandro. Soon Carlos Almeida welcomed me to the J. A. Freitas Library (JAF) and the Portuguese Union of the State of California (UPEC) Cultural Center to research the Portuguese contributions to the tiny hamlet of San Leandro on the San Francisco Bay.

The book is a tapestry of personal narratives from first-, second-, and third-wave Portuguese immigrants interwoven with material from Portuguese fraternal societies and excerpts from *Portuguese Immigrants: The Centennial Story of the Portuguese Union of the State of California* and Portuguese Heritage Publications of California; images used from this book are cited *Portuguese Immigrants*. I am grateful to all those in the community who opened up their places of business to meet with me, including Carlos Almeida from the J. A. Freitas Library and the librarians in the history room of the San Leandro Public Library. Images from the library are cited with the initials SLPLHPC. I would like to thank Katarina Ortega for her layout and formatting suggestions; my editor Kelly Reed for her assistance and support; my copy editor Lauren Bobier for her attention to detail; Devon Weston for her encouragement during the initial stages of the project; and Anne Tate for her assistance in the project's completion. I am especially grateful to Carlos Almeida from Uniao Portuguesa do Estado da California, who knows every book in the J. A. Freitas Library like the back of his hand. To any who submitted images or notations that do not appear here, I look forward to future publications. A portion of the proceeds from the sale of this book will be donated to the J. A. Freitas Library.

—Meg Rogers

INTRODUCTION

During the 15th century, Portuguese explorers circled the globe. In 1542, the Portuguese explorer Cabrilho explored the coast of Alta California, following the coast from San Diego up to the Santa Rosa and Santa Cruz islands. Even after the Age of Discovery slipped into decline, the spirit of exploration simmered.

More than 80 percent of Portuguese immigrants who came to the New World emigrated from the Azores islands, 814 nautical miles west of mainland Portugal. The volcanic Azorean islands were a natural stopping-over place for ships en route to the New World. Whaling ships passing through the Azorean islands of Pico and Faial lured Azoreans across the sea by promising them good wages, which would later enable them to send for their families back home. Leaving the port of Horta in Faial, Azorean immigrants swept over the sea to the New World, landing in Hawaii, Massachusetts, and along the California coast.

Portuguese immigration to California boomed when gold was discovered in 1848. The Portuguese came in large numbers, not to mine for gold, but to work in saloons and stores, which sprung up around the gold mining industry. The Portuguese were a practical people who soon realized that California had fertile ground for farming. They worked hard and bought up as much land as they could. After the Gold Rush, San Leandro and San Diego became a landing place for the Portuguese. Gradually, through thrift and hard work, Portuguese immigrants flourished, often calling their relatives from the Old World. Relatives in the Portuguese *colonias* of San Diego and San Leandro took care of each other, often helping newly arrived immigrant relatives obtain jobs and housing. Many Portuguese immigrants came to San Leandro through Hawaii. In San Leandro, the dream of home ownership denied to many Portuguese immigrants in Hawaii became a reality.

Portuguese settlers from the Azores brought with them the traditions of farming, festa, and family, transplanting the ancient Holy Ghost Festa and reinventing it to include St. Isabel's vision of feeding the poor. Like many Americans, the Portuguese immigrants in San Leandro were hit hard by the Great Depression. Some survived through subsistence farming. Others disillusioned by the failure to materialize the American dream returned home to their families in the Azores. There were many hurdles to overcome, and Portuguese immigrants often joined fraternal societies, which helped ease their transition to the New World. One such organization, the Portuguese Union of the State of California (UPEC), was founded in San Leandro in 1880 by an early group of Portuguese Catholics and Masons.

Interesting events in the Portuguese community of San Leandro included the cherry festival in June, which attracted people from all over California, and the Portuguese Holy Ghost Festa. Interesting characters include the first Catholic freemason members of UPEC; Helen Lawrence of Faial, America's first Portuguese mayor in the 1940s; and Carlos Almeida, secretary-treasurer of UPEC for 36 years and San Leandro City Library commissioner from 1966 to 1974. In 1964, Almeida founded the Joseph A. Freitas Portuguese library, which holds the largest collection of Portuguese documents, books, newspapers, and photographs of the Portuguese in California, dating back to the 1880s. Other notable people included the Mendonça family of farm workers turned landowners and community leaders, and Hal Peary, a third-generation descendent of immigrants from Faial, who was born in San Leandro in 1908 on Dabner Street and went on to be a famous television and movie star following his own enormously popular radio show: *The Great Gildersleeve.* Portuguese points of interest in San Leandro include the Irmandade Do Divino Espirito Santo (IDES) Hall, the J. A. Freitas Library and museum. Today the Portuguese Immigrant Monument in Root Park's windswept plaza commemorates the brave journey of the Portuguese settlers who left everything behind in hopes of being reborn in the New World.

One

PUTTING DOWN ROOTS

AZOREAN EMIGRANTS LEAVE FAIAL. Here Azorean emigrants leave Faial, Azores. At the turn of the century, the lure to cross the sea was powerful because Azores offered little in the way of economic or educational opportunity. A steady stream of Portuguese immigrants poured in from the Azores and mainland until 1924 when the INS enacted a quota system allowing only 440 Portuguese immigrants into the United States each year. John F. Kennedy thought the quota system was an injustice, and he fought for its elimination; he wanted immigration to be based on skill sets needed in America and not ethnicity. In 1964, after Kennedy's death, President Johnson signed Kennedy's bill lifting the unfair European immigration quotas. According to a study by Harvard professor Dr. Francis M. Rogers in 1970, there were 114,931 immigrants born in Portugal and the Azores residing in the United States. (Carlos Almeida.)

O Faial – Horta, o principal porto açoriano da baleação atlântica (séc. XVIII/XX).

HORTA PRINCIPAL PORT, FAIAL, AZORES. This painting by Benjamin Russell and Caleb Purrington depicts ships departing Faial. Portuguese immigrants journeyed across the Atlantic aboard whaling vessels bound for the New World. Life aboard the whaling vessels was dangerous and dreary with long hours and poor rations. Captains took advantage of the young Azorean workers who signed on with them—so much so that Azorean whalers often jumped ship to plow the fields of Hawaii and California. After the Gold Rush, San Leandro became one of the principal Portuguese settlements in the New World where immigrants worked on small farms and dairies. (Mar de Baleias by Joao Alfonso and *Portuguese Immigrants*.)

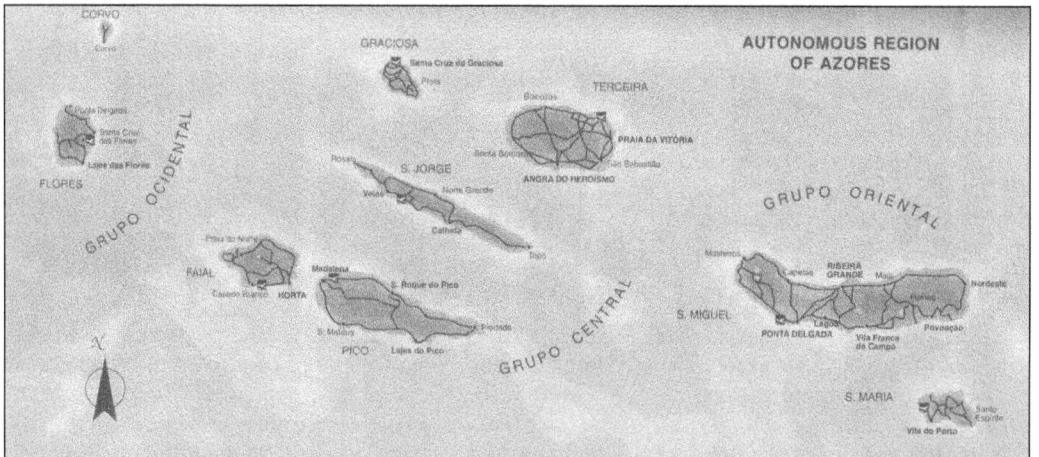

THE AZORES. More than 80 percent of Portuguese immigrants to San Leandro originally came from the Azores Islands, a mid-Atlantic chain 814 nautical miles out to sea from mainland Portugal. Plato's *Chrythias* describes the nine islands in the Azorean archipelago as peaks of mythical Atlantis. The Seven Cities Lake of San Miguel has two lakes in an ancient crater. Legend says when an Atlantean princess died, her shoes fell into one lake, which turned green, and her dress slipped into the other lake, which turned blue. (JAF.)

AZOREAN WHALERS, 1880S. This picture depicts the whaling fleet of Lages do Pico. One whaler holds his harpoon down while another points his short barrel shotgun at the camera. Many early Portuguese settlers made their way to California through the whaling industry. (Tony Wilson and Carlos Almeida.)

SAN MIGUEL WHALING STATION, 1920S. Factory workers cut a whale into vertical pieces before extracting its oil. Whale flesh was first put into cauldrons six feet in diameter, and then a wood fire was lit below, causing the fat and oil to rise to the top. Whale hunting supported many different industries: the oil was harvested for lighting, the teeth turned into ivory jewelry and artwork, and the remainder was used for pharmaceutical purposes. (*Portuguese Immigrants.*)

COMMERCIAL TRADE ROUTE MAP, 1902. This commercial map of the world from Frye's *Grammar School Geography*, 1902, shows turn-of-the-century rail and sea commercial shipping routes. Ships traveling across the Atlantic often stopped at Faial in the Azores for supplies and to recruit the young men living there who were known to be good whale hunters. Skilled whalers were in great demand to feed the ever-growing need for products made from whale oil, including flour, margarine, meat extracts, and soap. The whale-hunting route went from New Bedford across the Atlantic

into the West Indies around the Horn and on to the Pacific. Whalers signed two-year contracts to merciless captains who often kept them on deck, without leave, making them cut up and harvest whale oil onboard without seeing the shore for months on end. Fed up with the captain's slave-driving ways, many jumped ship, landing in Hawaii, Massachusetts, and along the California coast, sometimes under the captain's musket fire. (Alexis Frye, *Grammar School Geography*.)

PORTUGUESE SETTLERS IN HAWAII. Pictured at left is the 1938 portrait of Augusto Souza Costa. Below is Alexis Frye's 1902 map of the Hawaiian Islands. Costa was born in Terceira and educated in Hawaii. Costa worked as a store clerk in Honohina, Hawaii, until 1903, before coming to the mainland to work as a newspaperman for *O Reporter* in Oakland. Many Portuguese immigrants came to Hawaii to work in the sugar fields. They left when the Japanese immigrated and offered their services for a lower wage. Laid off, many Azoreans jumped ship again, landing in the Portuguese *colonia* of San Leandro, where they joined friends and family. Established Portuguese in San Leandro called these immigrants from Hawaii *kanakas*. *Kanakas* lived in tiny row houses on Orchard Avenue from Davis to Williams Street, an area that became known as Kanaka Row. (Carlos Almeida.)

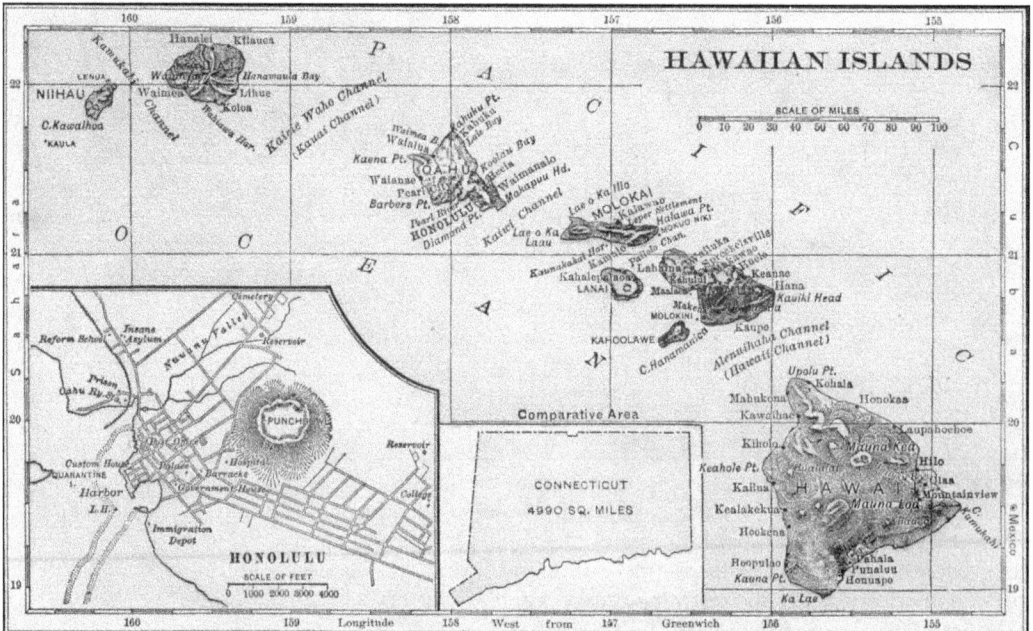

PORTUGUESE HAWAIIAN GARDEN AND HOLY GHOST CHAPEL. The picture above shows tourists visiting a Portuguese garden in the Iao Valley on Maui. Below is a photograph of the Holy Ghost Chapel on Punchbowl Hill on the island of Hawaii. JAS Webster, manager of the Pepeekeo Sugar Company, attributed the success of the Portuguese settlers in Hawaii to thrift and hard work. Portuguese settlers in Hawaii worked hard in hopes to purchase land; some even fashioned their own houses out of lava. Others left almost immediately for California. Those who stayed behind worked hard on plantations as field workers for $10 a month ($6 for women). In 1930, the Portuguese were the second-largest nationality in the territory of Hawaii, composing 29,117 of its 368,336 recorded residents. Many of the Portuguese immigrants to San Leandro came to California from the Western Islands (Azores) through the Sandwich Islands (Hawaii). (JAF, *Portuguese Hawaiian Memories.*)

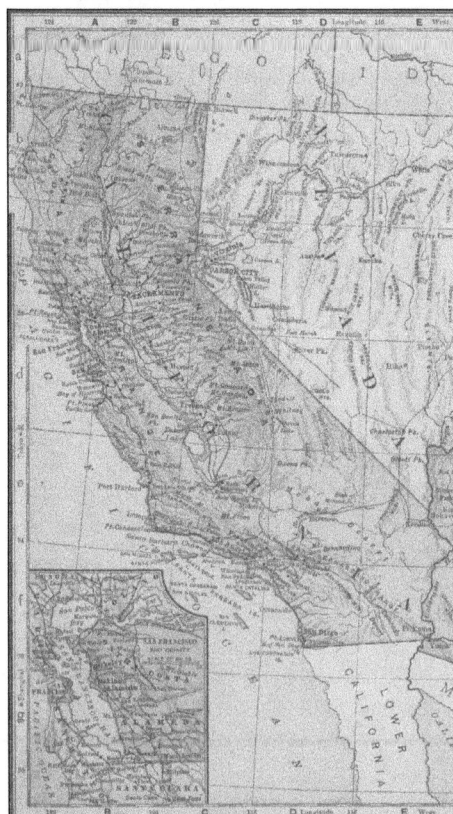

PORTUGUESE SETTLERS PUT DOWN ROOTS IN CALIFORNIA. Above is a ship from J. F. Freitas's *Portuguese Hawaiian Memories*; to the left is a 1902 map of California showing the Portuguese *colonia* of San Leandro. Abandoning Hawaiian sugar plantations, Portuguese settlers from Hawaii joined former Portuguese shore whalers, putting down roots along the California coast in San Leandro. Portuguese immigrants brought with them agricultural expertise gleaned from the sugar fields of Hawaii and hillside farming in the Azores. In Jack London's novel *Valley of the Moon*, he describes the innovations of the San Leandro's Portuguese farmers: "You think it growed that way, eh? Well, it did. But it was old Silva that made it just the same—caught two sprouts, when the tree was young, an' twisted 'em together. Pretty slick, eh? You bet. That tree'll never blow down. It's a natural, springy brace, an' beats iron braces stiff. Look along all the rows. Every tree's that way. See? An' that's just one trick of the Porchugeeze. They got a million like it." (JAF.)

CABRILHO. The monument pictured is a tribute to the Portuguese explorer Cabrilho and can be visited today in San Diego. In 1538, Cabrilho sailed under the Spanish crown first to South America and then up to Alta California. Cabrilho's vessel journeyed along the San Diego shore, going as far as the Santa Cruz and Santa Rosa Islands (see map on page 16). Cabrilho followed a long history of Portuguese exploration. In 1312, the Portuguese fought the enemies of Christianity expanding the Portuguese empire during the Age of Discovery. The 1400s brought further exploration under Portuguese Prince Henry's Military Order of the Christ and the Portuguese discovery of the Azores Islands, the point of origin for more than 80 percent of Portuguese immigrants to California. (JAF.)

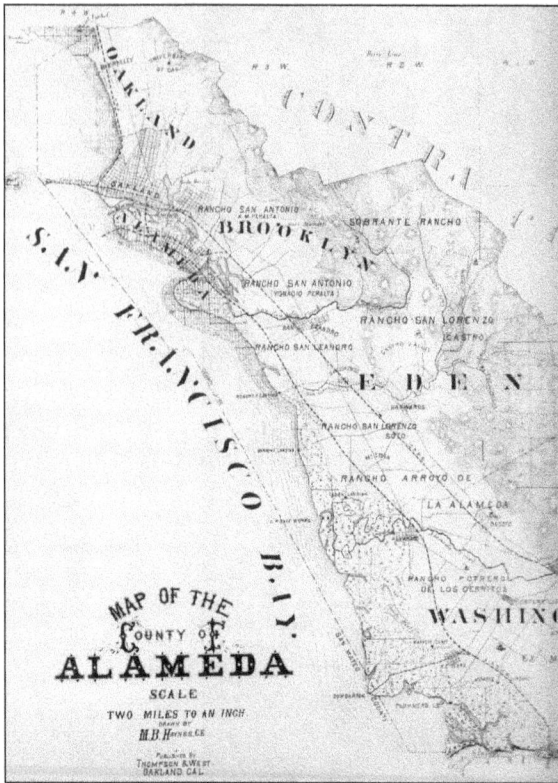

EDEN TOWNSHIP AND A TYPICAL PORTUGUESE FARMER. Shown to the left is an 1848 Alameda County map showing the boundaries of the Eden Township, which extend to the coastal range northeast and to the San Francisco Bay southwest. The township included the villages of San Leandro, Mount Eden, San Lorenzo, Andrews and Wicks Landings across the bay, Roberts Landing across from Haywood, and Eden Landing to the south. Eden Township was known for its farming implements, including the Sweepstakes and Eureka Gang Plows. The village of San Leandro at the junction of the Alameda and San Francisco Western Pacific Railroad lines served as Alameda's county seat from 1855 to 1873. Below a 1916 photograph shows Mel Dutra (on horse) and family posing outside their home on East Fourteenth Street, formerly Haywards Road. (Left M. B. Haynes Atlas, Thompson and West; below *Portuguese Immigrants*.)

MAP OF KANAKA ROW. At right, a map of San Leandro shows the boundaries of Kanaka Row: Pacific Street to the west, Alvarado Street to the east, Davis Street to the north, and Williams Street to the south. Kanaka Row derived its name from the nickname established Portuguese gave to Portuguese settlers from Hawaii. The other Portuguese enclave in San Leandro, Dutton Avenue, also known as Chicken Lane, is pictured above, c. 1890. Portuguese immigrants along Chicken Lane had thriving chicken farms. Portuguese women often served their own chickens for dinner and crocheted to let down at night. Their hobby was also practical; many Portuguese women made tablecloths and other lace items to give as presents. (JAF and SLPLHPC#2554.)

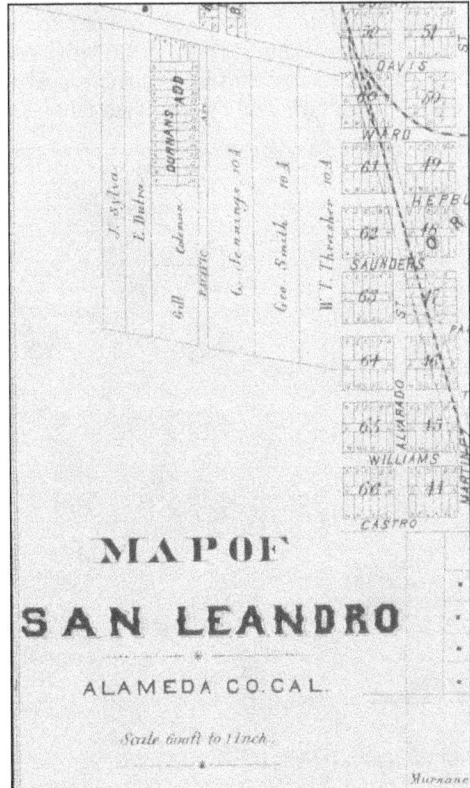

MAP OF

SAN LEANDRO

ALAMEDA CO. CAL.

Scale 600ft. to 1 inch

Murnane

ANDRADE FAMILY. Above an 1897 picture shows Harry Andrade and Louise Oakes Andrade in front of their family home. Below is a portrait Harry Andrade taken *c.* 1900. Andrade strolls along Dutton Avenue among eucalyptus trees planted in the 1850s. Early settlers to the Oakland area, including Thomas Mulford, got their land under the Squatter's Rights law, which divided Spanish ranchos into farms whose produce later fed nearby cities. (SLPLHPC#113 and #1110.)

FRONT GARDENS AND THE ANDRADE BOYS. Above Manuel Perry picks a bouquet of flowers from his front garden in Oakland to take to his relatives in San Leandro. Portuguese farmers were known for their front gardens, which often featured horse beans (fava beans). Portuguese farmers' houses could often be identified by their front and side gardens, which raised beans, a crop requiring a minimal amount of space in return for a high yield. San Leandro's fertile soil and mild climate allowed Azorean immigrant farmers to thrive—they worked every inch of their land, planting front gardens and developing innovative methods to yield the greatest crops. At right are William (left) and Henry Andrade (right). Born in 1888, William J. Andrade served as a sailor in 1920. (JAF and Anderson Lafler, "Alameda County: The Ideal Place for Your California Home," 1915.)

ANDRADE AND COSTA'S SALOON, 1899. Pictured left to right are Frank Fields, J. S. Costa, and J. J. Andrade behind the bar at Andrade and Costa's (Farmer's) Saloon located at 1166 East Fourteenth Street in San Leandro. The bar's signage advertised beers for 5¢ and a free lunch. The saloon was next door to Jose Olimpia's Grocery and Provisions, which later became the Luso-American Cooperative Mercantile Company. (Photograph by Stoddard, JAF.)

Two

DIVERSIFIED FIELDS
FARMING AND DAIRIES

FURNITURE MOVING VAN. Those identified in this photograph include Joe Silva in the back row, first from left, and Joe Freitas, fourth from left in the back. The motorcar was rented out to residents for picnics, hayrides, and the occasional move. Newly arrived Portuguese immigrants frequently moved from San Leandro to other *colonias* to join relatives who helped them obtain jobs and housing. Along with economic opportunity, educational opportunity was a big drive to come to America. Early Portuguese immigrants in San Leandro had low literacy rates. A 1911 U.S. Immigration Commission sample found that of 75 adult Portuguese residents sampled, more than half—38 of the 75—were illiterate. All 55 of the children sampled from the same households attending local schools were found to be literate. Although literacy rates were quite low among adults, home ownership rates were high. According to the U.S. Immigration Commission, many Portuguese immigrants achieved the American dream of home ownership. In 1911, exactly 31 out of the 36 Portuguese families sampled in San Leandro owned land. (JAF.)

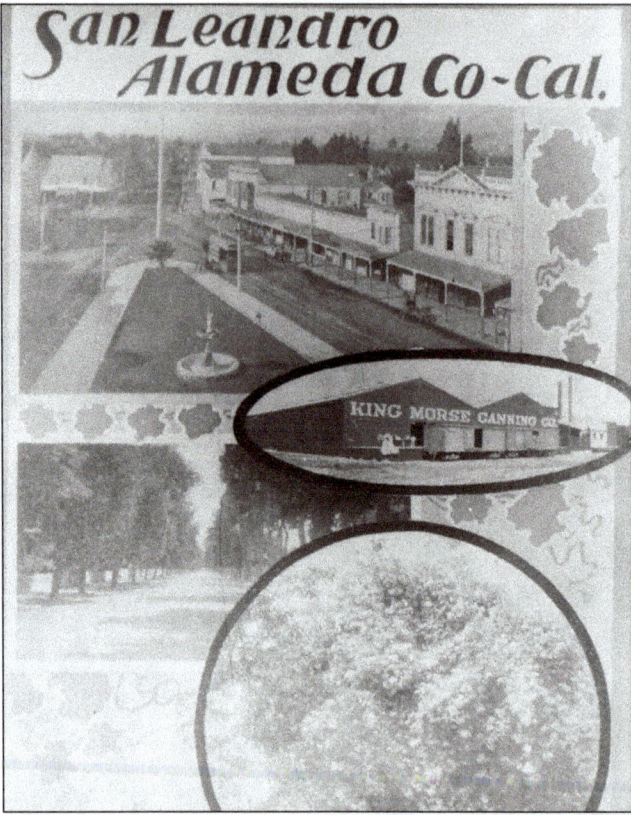

FARMING INNOVATIONS. The montage to the left shows Southern Pacific Station, the San Leandro Plaza (prior to 1906), and the cannery (dated *c.* 1899). Below is an 1890 photograph showing early San Leandro farmers taking produce to market. Portuguese settler J. B. Mendonça helped secure land to start the King Morse Cannery and bring it to San Leandro. Portuguese women and children often helped out around the farm during harvest time. The best fruit went to a farmer's exchange and the rest was sent to local canneries. Canned goods from San Leandro were shipped over the bay to San Francisco and then on to foreign ports. In 1910, the "San Francisco Call" Atlas estimated the value of canned vegetables and fruits shipped out of San Francisco to foreign ports at $289,788 and $1,795,890, respectively. (SLPLHPC#152.)

CANNERY ROW AND FARMHANDS. Mr. and Mrs. Tom Duffy (above) stand on the steps of San Lorenzo's California Preserving Company employee housing. Below picking peas at Mulford Gardens are, from left to right, Joe Moniz, John Coelho, and Frank Ignacio. Portuguese farmhands were prized for innovative planting techniques, including tripling an orchard's yield by planting two vegetable crops between the rows of trees. Jack London's 1913 novel *Valley of the Moon* describes San Leandro's Portuguese farmers: "They worked mornin', noon, an' night, all hands, women an' kids. Because they could get more out of twenty acres than we could out of a hundred an' sixty. Look at old Silva—Antonio Silva. I've known him ever since I was a shaver. He didn't have the price of a square meal when he hit this section and begun leasin' land from my folks. Look at him now--worth two hundred an' fifty thousan' cold, an' I bet he's got credit for a million, an' there's no tellin' what the rest of his family owns." (SLPLHPC#1289 and #349.)

25

SAN LEANDRO TOWN HALL AND PORTUGUESE GARAGE. The above picture dated between 1898 and 1908 shows San Leandro's town hall on Davis Street. Town hall was a favorite place for portraits of many kinds, including those of San Leandro's first fire squadron and early officers of the UPEC. To the left of town hall is Dennis Gleason's Blacksmith Shop next to Gallet's Livery Stable. Although most Portuguese immigrant settlers in San Leandro were farmers, a few worked in the trades, including William Edward Oakes and Joseph Sylva, who sold harnesses, and George Faria Sarmento, who worked as a blacksmith. William Oakes's father, Antone Sylva, was one of the town's earliest settlers. In 1861, Sylva purchased a 13.5-acre farm from John Haas, who had purchased the tract from of Ignacio Peralta. Below an unidentified Portuguese mechanic stands in front of a row of Ford automobiles at a Portuguese garage in San Leandro around 1912. (Bicentennial Collection of San Leandro and Carlos Almeida.)

MOTTA'S STORE. Manuel S. Motta's Grocery Store on East Fourteenth Street sold M. J. B. coffee and other provisions for a growing town. Many Portuguese immigrants worked in local supply stores after their arrival to the Portuguese *colonia* of San Leandro, including Manuel Bettencourt, who worked for Locke Brothers' Grocery Store in 1913, and Manuel Borge, who worked for Roberts Market in 1933. (Carlos Almeida, *Centennial Souvenir Album IDES* [CACSAIDES].)

ENOS' GROCERY, C. 1920. Pictured are Annie Lucio (left) and Adele Enos. Women and children often helped out on the farm and at family-run stores. (SLPLHPC#1938.)

J. F. Silva General Store, c. 1880s. A Portuguese clerk and patron stand inside of J. F. Silva's General Store on East Fourteenth Street. The store, which carried a variety of items, was adjacent to J. F. Silva's Saloon in San Leandro. A stained-glass advertisement for Blue and Gold Lager hangs above the saloon's entrance. (JAF.)

Olimpia Groceries, c. 1880s. Joseph Olimpia (right) stands in front of his store at East Fourteenth and Callan Streets, next to the UPEC hall in San Leandro. Olimpia's store later became the Luso-American Cooperative Mercantile Company, which sold dry goods and groceries. The co-op opened in 1873 and shut its doors in 1929. Andrade and Costa's Farmer's Saloon was next door. (Carlos Almeida.)

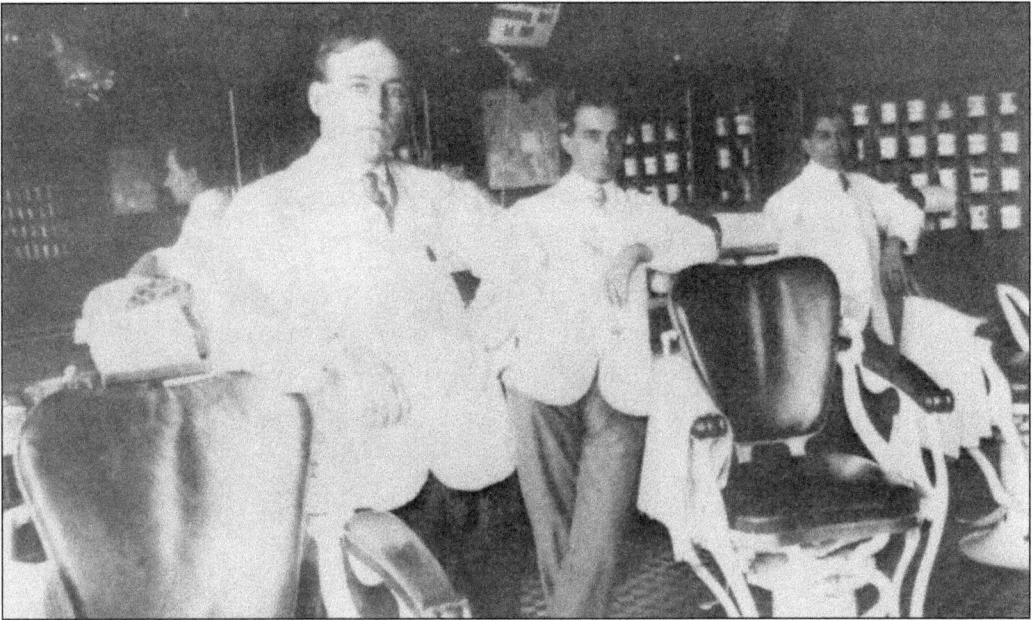

TWO BARBERSHOP PICTURES. The picture above, dated 1910, shows Mat Xavier in center next to two unidentified men. Xavier served as IDES of Alvarado Street's Holy Ghost secretary for several years. Holy Ghost Festas were a religious tradition, which helped Portuguese immigrants and their children preserve Portuguese culture in the New World. Below employees from Galvan's barbershop on East Fourteenth Street gather with local musicians for an impromptu party. Portuguese musicians often played local parties. At the turn of the century, San Leandro had many talented Portuguese musicians, including J. A. Freitas and Mario B. Camara, both of whom played in the UPEC's Uniform Rank band based in San Leandro. According to UPEC founder Antonio Fonte, the UPEC band formed in 1905 would not only "bring prestige to the society, but also a lot of publicity and no doubt attract the young generation." (Above, CACSAIDES and *Portuguese Immigrants*; below JAF.)

PHILLIP BROTHERS' DAIRY, SAN LEANDRO. Manuel Moitozo is pictured above with his team, delivering milk for Phillip Brother's Dairy, and is pictured below, fifth from the right, working on his own dairy in San Leandro. Moitozo had many jobs, including working at a foundry making Caterpillar truck parts and in Vallejo's hay fields. For Phillip Brother's in San Leandro, Moitozo drove a team from the breweries over to the dairies where he brought malt for the cattle. Moitozo saved his earnings, buying out the four partners one at a time. The proceeds of the dairy's sale in 1920 financed Moitozo's purchase of Moitozo Ranch in San Jose, which cost Moitozo $20,000 in gold bullion. Moitozo almost didn't make it to San Jose, nearly dying in the flu epidemic of 1918. Today Moitozo Park at Rio Robles and First Streets in San Jose commemorates the contributions of Portuguese settlers to the Bay Area. (Mac Moitozo.)

PLUMBING AND GAS FITTING WAGON. Joe A. Freitas (holding the reins, above) worked as a plumber's apprentice before purchasing a plumbing and garage company in Oakland, which he ran until 1955. UPEC president in 1924 and 1959, Freitas also toured as a musician with the UPEC band. Today the J. A. Freitas Library in San Leandro is dedicated to his memory. (JAF and *Portuguese Immigrants*.)

MULFORD FARM, 1937. George Mendonça plows Mulford's fields in San Leandro with a "gas-powered bull" (three-wheeled tractor). George Mendonça's father, J. B. Mendonça, worked from 1868 to 1873 as a laborer for Mulford before becoming Mulford's foreman, which helped Mendonça purchase 30 acres in San Leandro in 1876. San Leandro's bicentennial committee attributed Mendonça's success to his many business ventures, including trade and passenger shipping, oyster beds, hunting, farming, and dairy and hotel operations. (SLPLHPC#16.)

WATER WAGON, 1890. Pictured on the Mulford farm are, from left to right, J. B. Mendonça, Ira Mendonça, an unidentified cousin, Arthur Mendonça, Mae Lewis, and Joe Lewis. The Mendonça Ranch water wagon was very successful in the East Bay at the time. Today Mendonça's legacy has all but disappeared. In 1972, the last part of the Mendonça family's acreage was converted into an industrial area along Marina Boulevard. (Carlos Almeida, JAF, and SLPLHPC#20.)

BEST'S ELECTRIC CRUDE OIL VAPOR ENGINE, 1897. Pictured here is Daniel Best's invention, an engine that ran on different types of fuel: kerosene, distillate, crude oil, or gasoline. Best's engine was awarded the state fair prize of first premium in 1890. Best was a great inventor with more than 41 patents to his name. Best's C. L. Best Manufacturing Company later merged with Holt to become Caterpillar. Daniel Best employed many of San Leandro's Portuguese immigrants. (SLPLHPC#1590.)

BEST BUILDING, C. 1911. Above is an early picture of the Daniel Best Building on the corner of Estudillo Avenue. According to *A Saga of San Leandro*, the lower floor's wainscoting and the Hayward and Estudillo Avenue stairway entrances were constructed from solid Alaskan marble. The building later became Bank of America. (*Portuguese Immigrants.*)

BEST MANUFACTURING COMPANY, 1895. Pictured above is Daniel Best sitting in the center chair. Best employed many of San Leandro's Portuguese residents, including Joe Focha and Joe Freitas in 1897. Daniel Best's business ventures included building two automobiles: a two-seater and a ten-seater. Today Best's cars are pretty rare: only four were sold in 1895, sixteen in 1896, ninety in 1897, eight hundred in 1898, three thousand two hundred in 1899, and eight thousand in 1900. Best once said, "I have often thought if I had stayed with automobile manufacturing I could have out-Forded Ford." (SLPLHPC#224 and *Daniel Best, a Biography*.)

BORMAN'S GROCERY NEAR THE PLAZA. The two men in the above picture are unidentified. Borman's Grocery was known for its excellent selection. Many Portuguese immigrants worked for local grocery stores and creameries delivering groceries and milk to local patrons with horse-drawn wagons. (SLPLHPC#340.)

JOSEPH HERRSCHER'S STORE, C. 1900. Here pictured from left to right are Joseph Herrscher, Mrs. Herrscher, Sam Jacobs, Henry Costa, and Tony Brillo. Joseph Hersher and Louis Borman both joined the UPEC in 1892, the first year the Portuguese fraternal society allowed non-Portuguese members. (SLPLHPC#1991 and *Portuguese Immigrants*.)

34

T. B. MORGAN GROCERY STORE, C. 1911. Morgan's store was on East Fourteenth Street near city hall. Pictured here from left to right are Tom Morgan, Frank Gonsalves, and Alonzo Ferreira. Gonsalves led "the Little German Band" in the 1911 cherry festival, which took place from June third to the fifth. (SLPLHPC#484)

ROBERTS MARKET. Pictured here from left to right are the following: (first row) Budd Eber, the butcher behind the counter; William Mathews; two unidentified people; Ellie Roberts; (second row) Ed Horne; Lawrence Roberts; Stanley Haleian; Marie Roberts; Manuel Borge. Both Eber and Borge participated in San Leandro's cherry festival of 1912—Eber as parade director and Borge as a grand marshal. (SLPLHPC#120.)

HOME DELIVERY, 1907. Posing on East Fourteenth Street are, from left to right, Manuel Andrade, Frank Gonsalves (with reigns), and Joseph Oakes, standing. The wagon's letters read "organ," so the delivery was probably for Morgan's Grocery Store on Davis Street. In 1915, when Manuel Joseph Andrade Jr. was postmaster, there were plans to make San Leandro the third city in California with free mail delivery, but the plans fell through and San Leandro's post office became branch "H" of Oakland's Post Office until 1937. (SLPLHPC#550.)

FIRST AUTO MEAT DELIVERY TRUCK, 1912. This picture, taken on Washington Avenue, shows Harry Eber driving San Leandro's first auto meat delivery truck. Many Portuguese immigrants transported meat and milk for local Portuguese dairies. Portuguese dairymen established cooperatives to protect their collective interests, including San Francisco's Associated Milk Producers and Oakland's American Creamery Company, which was founded by Joaquim Silveira in 1899. (SLPLHPC#149.)

36

CREAMERY DELIVERY TRUCK. Here ? Hirschmann (left) and ? Gomes deliver milk for San Leandro Creamery. In 1912, the creamery's foot traffic boomed when the first public telephone was put in next door at the Masonic lodge. (SLPLHPC#709.)

EBER'S MEAT MARKET, BETWEEN 1908 AND 1912. The two identified men in this Eber's Meat Market photograph are Budd Eber, second from left, and Harry Eber, third from left. Despite the Gurney Refrigerating Company sign behind the men, some of the meat was not refrigerated; here the sausages and meat hang in open air. (SLPLHPC#57.)

TWO VIEWS OF THE BAY. Above is a view of the Alameda Estuary. Sometimes Portuguese fishermen homesick for the Azores would take little crafts out on the estuary. Fishing was a big pastime for the Azoreans, not only as a source of food but also for relaxation. Whaling expeditions knew of the Azorean talent for spearing fish and would often try to lure them into whale hunting. Fishing was the occupation of several early Portuguese immigrants in San Leandro, including Antonio Leanco Ferreira, who was a fish dealer. Below is a picture of pile driving at Mulford Landing taken around 1910. The Portuguese played an active role in dredging the marina. J. Focha, along with Arthur Mendonça, Manuel Serpa, and Antone Souza, worked together to dig irrigation ditches in the San Leandro Marina using horses and donkeys. Irrigation ditches were necessary to drain water from the Mulford flats into the San Francisco Bay. (SLPLHPC#1847 and #45.)

OYSTER HARVEST IN SAN LEANDRO C. 1890. This picture shows workers using rakes to gather oysters. The man on the left is guarding the barge against oyster pirates. Author Jack London, who described the Portuguese immigrants of San Leandro in his novel, *Valley of the Moon*, worked as a member of the fish patrol after his youthful stint as an oyster pirate. (SLPLHPC#468.)

Where fried oysters first beg 1900

shack at oyster Mulford Sm

FRIED OYSTERS, C. 1900. The picture above shows the oyster shack at Mulford Landing's oyster beds in San Leandro. The picture reads, "where fried oysters first begin." Workers sit on top of the oyster shack at Mulford Landing. Many goods were shipped out of Mulford Landing to markets in San Francisco. (SLPLHPC#706.)

UNION HOSE COMPANY (1898) AND FIREFIGHTERS (1914). Above San Leandro's all-volunteer fire squadron poses at city hall. Pictured from left to right are the following: two unidentified men, Manuel Valence, Jim Cahill, Lou Whitcomb, Charlie Blankenship, Henry Bormann, John Gill, Bert Rogers, August Von Glahn, two unidentified people on the cart, George Bormann, Ed Whitcomb, Manuel Freitas, Harry Eber, John Bigelow, and John Voght, who was fire chief from 1899 to 1910. Those in the background are unidentified. Behind the fire squadron is their hose cart and single-cylinder gas pump. Volunteer firefighters received $15 annually for their services. Below, standing in front of San Leandro's first fire apparatus in 1914 are, from left to right, the following: (first row) George Bormann; Henry Bormann; Manuel Freitas; police chief Joseph Peralta, and fire chief Budd Eber; (second row) Bert Rodgers and Chris Hopper, the driver. (SLPLHPC#513 and #1198.)

FIRE AT INTERCOASTAL PAINT. This modern picture shows San Leandro Fire Department's quick response to a fire at Intercoastal Paint. Residents weren't always so fortunate. In 1872, on Dutton Avenue (Chicken Lane) slightly outside the city limits, Vincent Cardoz made firecrackers for the Holy Ghost Festa. A pipe was lit, and his powder keg set ablaze. Medical aid was called for but none arrived, and Cardoz's infant child died shortly after the explosion. (SLPLHPC#37.)

FIRE DEPARTMENT, 1926. Included in the picture Manuel Agrella, August Thystn, Arthur "Bat" Larsen, Serafino Toti, Archie Souza, Manuel Freitas, Sill Godchaux, George Borman, Chris Hopper (driving), Joseph Francisco Peralta Jr., Joe Peralta Sr. (Ygnacio Peralta's grandson), Manuel Freitas, Budd Eber (wearing glasses), Thommy Stevans, Walter Iversen, Lee Martin, Clarence Avelar, Charley Wright, ? Miller, Herbert Landis, and O. F. Chichester. (SLPLHPC#495.)

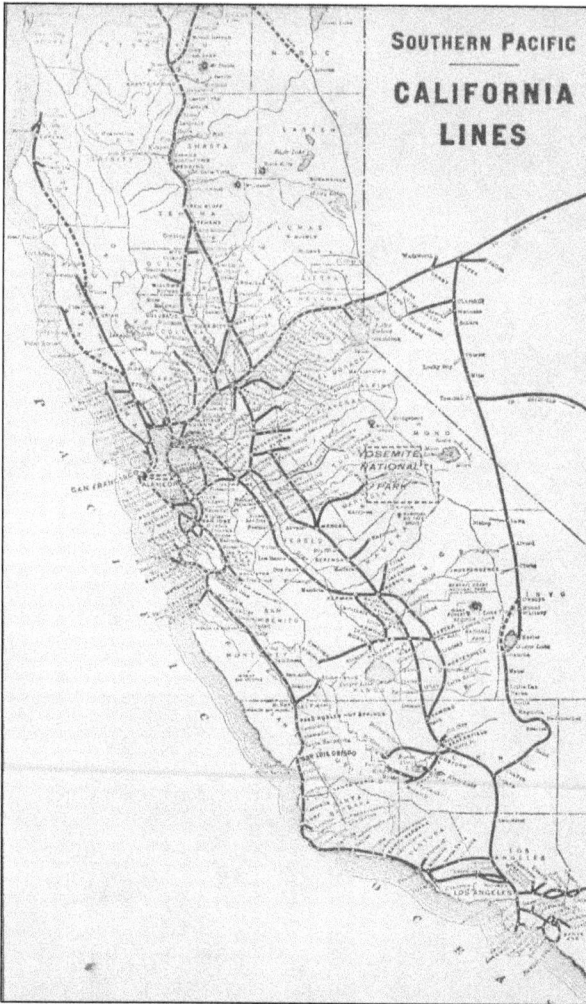

BUILDING THE RAILROAD. To the left is a map showing the Southern Pacific Railroad lines in California. Before the railroads, produce was shipped to market in San Francisco out of Mulford Landing, where it traveled by boat to San Francisco before being shipped abroad. In 1892, Southern Pacific introduced refrigerated railroad cars, which made shipping fresh produce to other parts of the country a breeze. As seen below, many Portuguese immigrants also worked for Western Pacific Railroads. Here an unidentified worker lays ties for the new tracks near Davis and Alvarado Streets in San Leandro. Many Portuguese immigrants came to work for Southern Pacific in Oakland because they had friends and family in the area, including Manuel Medeiros from San Miguel. Medeiros worked for Southern Pacific before becoming the leader of the UPEC band, which played many concerts in the Bay Area, including in San Leandro. (Carlos Almeida and SLPLHPC#369.)

ELECTRIC RAILWAY, 1882, FIRST DAY OF SERVICE. The Oakland, San Leandro, and Hayward Electric Railway Car No. 30 gave free rides to children on its first day of operation on May 7, 1892. (Bicentennial Collection of San Leandro and Carlos Almeida.)

WILLIAM ANDRADE AT OAKLAND DEPOT, 1907. Pictured third from the left is William J. Andrade at Oakland's Sixteenth Street Railroad Depot. According to Portuguese historian Alvin Graves, job opportunities at Central Pacific Railroad led to a surge in West Oakland's Portuguese population, which tripled from 10,500 in 1870 to 34,555 in 1880. Many Portuguese immigrants who settled in Oakland had friends or family in San Leandro. (JAF and Alvin Graves.)

JOSEPH MENDONÇA FLOAT, 1909. Here the J. B. Mendonça cherry festival float travels by horse and carriage down East Fourteenth Street between Juana and Joaquim Avenues, in front of where the Bank of America stands today. In 1868, Joseph Bernardo Mendonça left Faial and sailed through the Isthmus of Panama, landing in San Francisco and moving to San Leandro to lease 1,000 acres from Don Francisco Peralta. After farming for three years, Mendonça saved enough to buy the 200-acre Mulford Ranch near the marina in San Leandro. Mendonça's float joined many others in the cherry festival parade. San Leandro's cherry festival of 1909 had a huge turnout. On May 29, 1909, the *San Leandro Reporter* ran an advertisement for the upcoming festival: "San Leandro Cherries Free on June 5th: Many Thousand Strangers Will Avail Themselves of this Grand Opportunity of Visiting San Leandro and Partake of Harvest's Choicest Fruit. And Entertainment is Arranged that will Surpass any ever before Attempted." (Carlos Almeida, "San Leandro Recollections," Vol 3, No. 6, 1972.)

44

Three

FLOATS, FESTAS, AND PARADES

CHERRY FESTIVAL, 1922. Queen Gladys Madeira poses with her royal court after claiming her prize, a $125 genuine diamond ring. Her male attendant was Manuel Bettencourt, and her maids of honor were Victoria Duarte, Elanor Federighi, Hyacinth Gonsalves, Leona Duarte, Ida Olympia, Evelyn Valance, and Dolores Breeves. The first cherry queen in the city of San Leandro was Bessie Best. The second cherry queen was Mabel Furtado, a young lady of Portuguese descent. The cherry festival delighted out-of-towners and residents alike with its magnificent parades and beautiful floats. San Leandro had a cherry festival every year from 1909 to 1912. After a 10-year hiatus, the festivals resumed in 1922, continuing each year until 1931. The most notable of San Leandro's modern cherry festivals took place during San Leandro's bicentennial in 1972. (Carlos Almeida and JAF.)

OAKLAND TRIBUNE CHERRY FESTIVAL ADVERTISEMENT. This advertisement from the *Oakland Tribune* features a lovely old-fashioned woman leaning on a cherry branch. It reads, "The Citizens of San Leandro cordially invite the general public to be their guests on this happy day and participate in the festivities of this gala occasion. Lucious Cherries Free." (Herman Ilene, *Cherry Festivals of the Past.*)

CHERRY FESTIVAL, 1915. Carrie Dutra drives this car covered with cherries to celebrate the festival. Behind her is a cherry orchard in San Leandro. The automobile's wheels have been decorated with the colors of the American flag. (JAF.)

QUEEN MABEL. At right is a 1910 portrait of Mabel Furtado; pictured below at the head of the table, Furtado attends a dinner in her honor. In 1910, Furtado was voted San Leandro's cherry festival queen through a newspaper ballot in San Leandro and Oakland papers. According to *The Saga of San Leandro*, Furtado lost the popular vote when Virgie Wilson stuffed the ballot box the last day with votes from friends and family. After a heated discussion with *San Leandro Reporter* owner William Zambresky, Furtado was given the title of queen. Wilson withdrew from the competition and was refunded $600 worth of ballots. On June, 10, 1910, Furtado was crowned queen at 10:30 a.m. on San Leandro's plaza bandstand. A huge parade followed with cars and floats decorated with thousands of cherries and bows. Free cherries were available to all. The day's festivities also included the Eden Township baseball game, San Leandro versus Hayward, and a marathon of 18 miles. (JAF.)

CHERRY CARNIVAL, JULY 4, 1892. The Fourth of July float of 1892 boasted real cherries. The identified members of this photograph include George Helms, Edward Tenny, Dorothy Begier, Minnie Begier Lindsey, Harry Begier (on ladder), and driver Tommy Johnson. The girls, listed from left to right, are Ellie Moldenhauer, Minnie Begier, and unidentified. Standing from left to right are Odella Heinaka, ? Moldenhauer, John Henry Begier, and Mr. and Mrs. Henry Moldenhauer; Seated on the bench in no particular order are Edward Tenny, Jack Dumont, Joel Burrows, Mrs. J. H. Begier, Ben Begier, James Whitcomb, Louis Reithrath, Douglas Toffelmier, Tom Sturdevant, and Edward Whitcomb. Seated on the ground from left to right are ? Grile, Manuel Enos, Eugene Toffelmier, John Mendell, Mike Gorman, and Hugh Gillespie. Reclining in front are George Ferria and Billie the dog. The little girl is unidentified. (Budd Eber and SLPLHPC#125.)

LATE 1800S MARDI GRAS BAND. This picture, c. 1890, shows San Leandro's Portuguese Mardi Gras dance group, Danca de Carnaval. The Portuguese community celebrated Mardi Gras with live music. Many of the participants came in costume. (JAF.)

CHERRY FESTIVAL IN SAN LEANDRO, 1912. This picture, taken at the intersection of East Fourteenth and Davis Streets, shows the cherry queen of 1912, Mable Duetsch. The maids from left to right are M. Mason, Bessie Birchenal, and Frances Michael. Aids to the queen are driver Manuel Garcia and, on horseback, grand marshal Ferdinand "Budd" Eber. (Budd Eber and JAF.)

CHERRY FESTIVAL CARNIVAL. This picture shows the cherry festival in full swing. Also visible are the Herrscher Building and globe streetlights. Though the picture is dated c. 1915, other sources date this picture in the 1920s; the 1915 date seems unlikely because that year, San Leandro's cherry festival committee agreed to accept the invitation from the Panama Pacific International Exhibition to hold the festival in San Francisco on June 10th at the exhibition. There was talk of holding a festival in town following the exhibition, but nothing came of it. (SLPLHPC#163.)

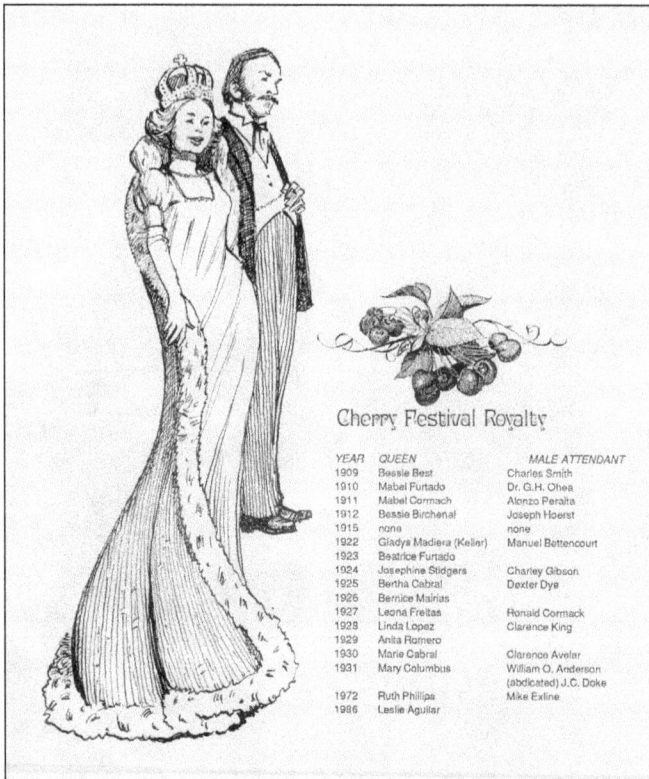

Cherry Festival Royalty

YEAR	QUEEN	MALE ATTENDANT
1909	Bessie Best	Charles Smith
1910	Mabel Furtado	Dr. G.H. Ohea
1911	Mabel Cormach	Alonzo Peralta
1912	Bessie Birchenal	Joseph Hoerst
1915	none	none
1922	Gladys Madeira (Keller)	Manuel Bettencourt
1923	Beatrice Furtado	
1924	Josephine Stidgers	Charley Gibson
1925	Bertha Cabral	Dexter Dye
1926	Bernice Mairias	
1927	Leona Freitas	Ronald Cormack
1928	Linda Lopez	Clarence King
1929	Anita Romero	
1930	Marie Cabral	Clarence Avelar
1931	Mary Columbus	William O. Anderson (abdicated) J.C. Doke
1972	Ruth Phillips	Mike Exline
1986	Leslie Aguilar	

CHERRY COURT. This drawing from Herman Ilene's *Cherry Festivals of the Past* depicts a prototypical cherry queen and her male attendant. San Leandro had numerous Portuguese cherry queens, including Mabel Furtado in 1910 and Gladys Madeira in 1922. When the festival was in its prime, San Leandro was booming with cherries, peaches, apricots, lemons, hay, and tomatoes. (Herman Ilene's *Cherry Festivals of the Past.*)

CHERRY COMMITTEE LETTER. Pictured at right is a fund-raising letter of San Leandro's 1910 Cherry Festival Committee. On April 24, 1909, the cherry festival committee decided to put up a queen for the festival. Voting was held at Holmgren's store and cost 1¢. The following were the cherry queen contestants: Bessie Best, Mary Burroughs, Bessie Bradwell, Mabel Cormack, Mabel Furtado, Mary Gonsalves, Mildred Hawes, Emma Herrscher, Alice Locke, Catherine McCoy, Hazel Reid, Grace Rideout, Vivian Santos, Madeline Silva, and Alice Stewart. Best won her crown with 3,894 votes. (JAF.)

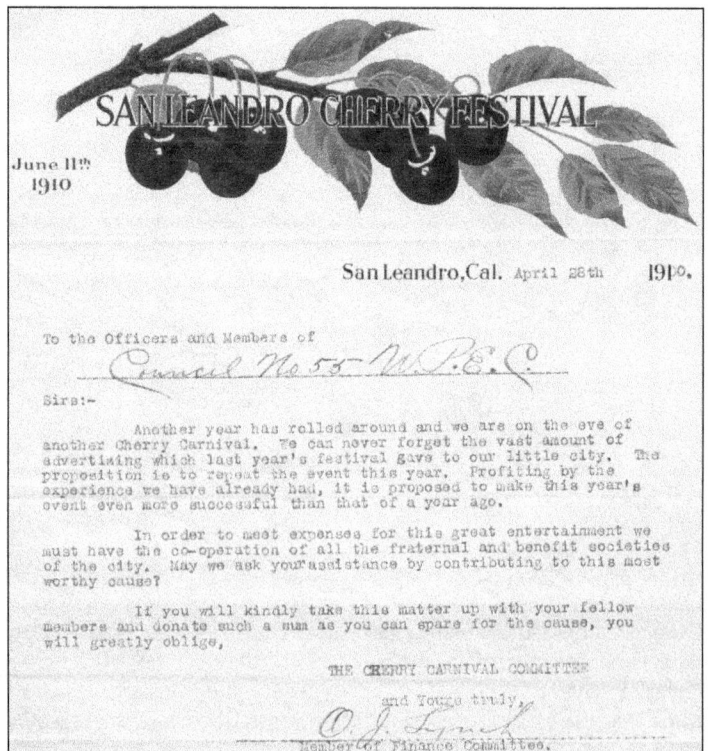

CHERRY COURT. This picture shows the crowning of the first cherry queen Bessie Best, center, and ladies in waiting Alice Locke on the left and Mabel Furtado on the right. The coronation of the queen took place at 10:30 a.m. and was followed by 15 tons of free cherries, a baby parade, a baseball game, free concerts, and a ball at the UPEC Hall. Forester's Band, which provided entertainment, had several Portuguese members, including Joe Bettencourt, George Rogers, Joaquin Silva, Tony Bettencourt, Manuel Nunes, Frank Gonsalves, Frank Rogers, Manuel Freitas, and Bill Rogers. (*Saga of San Leandro* and JAF.)

CHERRY FESTIVAL, 1909. Pictured here from left to right are Alice Locke, the 1909 Cherry Festival queen Bessie Best, and Mabel Furtado, who was crowned queen the next year. Each June, the cherry festival was held in the downtown plaza on the corner of East Fourteenth and Davis Streets. The Best family founded the steam engine in 1888 and the Best Manufacturing Company later developed, along with Holt, into the Caterpillar Tractor Company. Portuguese farmers contributed cherries to decorate elaborate floats, which featured live cherries atop old Ford Cars and other contraptions. (JAF.)

CHERRY FESTIVAL QUEEN. Princess Myrtle Oakes (left), queen Mabel Furtado (center), and Alzina Demont pose at Furtado's house after her coronation as San Leandro's cherry queen of 1910. Pictured next to Furtado is Dr. G. H. Ohea. A crowd of 45,000 traveled from far and wide to see the spectacle. The second cherry festival was a huge boon to the city, drawing in tons of advertising dollars and showcasing its rich agricultural bounty. (JAF.)

UPEC FLOAT, 1910. Pictured here is the UPEC float of 1910, the year in which Mabel Furtado was named queen. The Furtados were especially proud of their young cherry queen and decorated the house with a sign that read, "Queen Mabel." The 1910 cherry festival events spanned three days, starting Friday night with dancing in the streets, live bands, an electric light show, and a ball in honor of Queen Mabel at the Masonic lodge. (JAF.)

FIRST SETTLERS, SAN LEANDRO CHERRY FESTIVAL PARADE, 1925. Pictured here in the first car, from left to right, are San Leandro Portuguese residents Aurora Perry, Mrs. John Abrew, Gertrude Higuera, and John Rodrigues. They are celebrating the contributions of Portuguese settlers to San Leandro as they ride in their old Ford during the cherry festival. (JAF.)

SAN LEANDRO BALL CLUB DURING CHAMBER OF COMMERCE WEEK. Those identified include Isabelle Vierra (center) and N. W. Armstrong (kneeling third from the left in front). The chamber of commerce strongly supported the annual cherry festival. In *A Garden Grows in Eden*, historian Harry Shaffer quotes the chamber's 1911 cherry festival essay contest winner, Querdon Sitton: "If Adam had lived in Eden Township, he never would have eaten the forbidden fruit, because he would have preferred San Leandro cherries." (SLPLHPC#353.)

FOURTH OF JULY PARADE. J. A. Freitas sits in the driver's seat on the Fourth of July parade in San Leandro. The car is decorated with the American flag and with red, white, and blue flowers in the spokes. (JAF.)

UPPEC DRILL TEAM, 1930. The Portuguese Protected Union State of California (UPPEC) drill team poses at the plaza fountain downtown San Leandro. The drill team took part in civic parades throughout California. Two decades earlier, in 1915, the UPEC gave all the UPPEC delegates attending the Portuguese fraternal convention in Oakland free tickets to the Panama Pacific International Exhibition. Many Portuguese residents in San Leandro attended the exhibition, decorating their automobiles to receive free admission. (*Portuguese Immigrants.*)

Four

UPEC/EXCURSIONS AND FAIRS

UPEC OFFICERS IN FRONT OF CITY HALL ON DAVIS STREET, 1888. From left to right are Carl Iversen, Joseph Bettencourt, Manuel Andrade, Manuel Rodgers, Jesse Woods, Joseph Olympia, Manuel Braga, Joe Barbara, and Manuel Avilla. The UPEC was founded in 1880 to protect Portuguese immigrants by providing assistance to them when they fell ill or had an untimely death in the family. The preamble to the constitution of the UPEC (Uniao Portuguesa do Estado da California) reads: "We the undersigned declare that we met in assembly and from our own free will unanimously adopted this constitution of the society 'Portutguese Union' as the first founders. Praise to the Lord so that we progress and serve as an example and memorial for the future of our sons and compatriots; and when we no longer exist, be it known to all men, that the purpose of this society 'Portuguese Union' is for the benefit of our homeland, heritage, honor and glory of our Portuguese nationality." (*Portuguese Immigrants.*)

INITIATION TEAM. Pictured above is UPEC's Vasco da Gama initiation team. According to Carlos Almeida, the UPEC was a unique organization in its day uniting "all Portuguese immigrants and their descendants, regardless of their political or religious convictions. Birthplace was also disregarded. Continentals, Madeirans, and Azoreans put clannish feelings aside and united to assist each other in the conquest of respect in the strange land of America." (*Portuguese Immigrants.*)

SECRET BALLOT. In 1892, non-Portuguese Caucasians were permitted to join the UPEC provided that they agreed to an inspection of their character by the investigating committee and a brotherhood vote by secret ballot. Three black balls (shown to the left) could prohibit membership. Prior to 1887, potential members had to speak Portuguese; after the language requirements were dropped, potential members only had to prove they had good morals and good social and moral character. (*Portuguese Immigrants.*)

UPEC HEADQUARTERS. The first UPEC office was located at what is today the UPEC hall in San Leandro. Lucindo Martins, seated at left, was state treasurer, and Mario B. Camara, center, was the founder and leader of the original UPEC band, which played at the Panama Pacific Exposition in San Francisco in 1915. Manuel Bettencourt, right, was assistant secretary-treasurer. On the bottom left is an old spittoon for guests. (*Portuguese Immigrants.*)

ST JOSEPH'S, 1880S. St. Joseph's Hall on Davis Street was the original location of the first UPEC meetings. In 1880, thirty Portuguese immigrants signed the UPEC constitution at St. Joseph's Hall and elected UPEC's first officers, including Antonio Fonte (president), Victorino Theodoro Braga (vice president), Jose Maria Telles (secretary), William Dutra Smith (treasurer), and Victorino Jose de Braga (finance committee). (JAF and *Portuguese Immigrants.*)

MARIO B. CAMARA. Lucio da Silva Gonsalves immigrated to San Francisco in 1892, taking a newspaper job with *Uniao Portuguesa*. Camara had been instrumental in the overthrow of Portuguese monarchy in 1889 and was part of the movement that established the Republic of Portugal. To ensure his saftey in the New World, Lucio da Silva took the new name of Mario B. Camara. (*Portuguese Immigrants.*)

SUPREME OFFICERS AND DIRECTORS OF THE UPEC. Pictured from left to right are the following: (first row) F. I. Lemos, M. Fraga, F. E. Pinheiro, Frank Lazarus, Frank S. Roderick, and Thomas F. Lopes; (second row) M. B. da Camara, J. A. Freitas, Alberto Moura, F. A. Freitas, J. T. Lopes, Joe M. Clemente, and J. J. Pimentel. (*Portuguese Immigrants.*)

UPEC HALL, 1168 EAST FOURTEENTH STREET, 1890. UPEC members from San Leandro join members from Hayward, Hollister, and Petaluma for UPEC's annual convention. Identified in the back row are third from the left Antonio G. Mattos, a former UPEC president and a state senator (Mattos was the first first-generation immigrant elected to the California State Legislature); fourth from the left is Antonio Fonte; unidentified; Francisco I. Lemos, founder of the Portuguese American Bank in San Francisco with branches in Los Banos, Oakland, and Newman; and Jose Pimentel (white beard), a mason who introduced Masonic rites to the UPEC and a justice of the peace in Hayward. No one could attend UPEC's convention without a tie, but most members were farmers who didn't own ties. Assistant secretary-treasurer Camara had a trunk at the door full of straight and bow ties so members could choose one before entering the session hall. (*Portuguese Immigrants.*)

UPEC HOME OFFICE, PURCHASED IN 1909. This picture shows the UPEC home office on East Fourteenth Street. In 1909, UPEC purchased the building for $4,000 from A. Rogers. The UPEC band played the "Star-Spangled Banner" at the building's dedication ceremony on September 12, 1909. In the building's cornerstone were placed several symbolic items, including five kings (Portuguese currency) dated 1880, the year UPEC was founded; copies of local English and Portuguese newspapers dated September 12, 1909; an 1880 silver dollar; and a picture of UPEC founder Antonio Fonte. (*Portuguese Immigrants.*)

PANORAMA OF THE PANAMA PACIFIC EXHIBITION AND UPEC CONVENTION, 1915 (BOTH PAGES). The aerial view above shows the Panama Pacific Exhibition in San Francisco. The Portuguese Pavilion at the exhibition was built in a Gothic style. After the exhibition, everything was dismantled except for the Palace of Fine Arts. Some of the pavilion's columns were incorporated into Joaquim Silveira's house in Oakland. Before the fair, the UPEC had its annual convention

in Oakland (below). At the time of the fair, the exposition wanted to feature Portugal, but the Portuguese government, which had just changed from a monarchy to a republic, was not willing to finance building the pavilion for the Portuguese exhibit. Three Portuguese from California—Dr. Jose Bettencourt, Joaquim Silveira, and Francisco I. Lemos—went to Portugal on June 15, 1914, to convince the Portuguese government to contribute to the fair. (JAF.)

PORTUGUESE PAVILION, PANAMA PACIFIC EXPOSITION, 1915. Above in the foreground is the Court of Abundance, where Portuguese Day was held. Below is the dedication ceremony of the Portuguese Pavilion. According to Portuguese historian August Vaz, UPEC's band gave a concert during the event, which gathered all the Portuguese fraternal societies in the Bay Area. The concert included Mozart, Wagner, and Canto's military march, the "Lusitano." The concert also featured a hymn composed for the fair by Fr. Candido Ribeiro with lyrics by Joao C. Valim. The hymn started, "*Pavilhao Portugues...Das gloriosas conquistas do mar...O retrato da Patria saudemos, Exclamando com alma: benvindo,*" which means, "The Portuguese Pavilion honors Portuguese maritime conquests, presenting a beautiful portrait to the world of our country's longing and its soul." After the UPEC's 80-piece band played its two-hour concert at the Court of Abundance, the crowd adjourned to watch fireworks at the marina. (JAF and *Portuguese Immigrants*.)

UPEC BAND AT PORTUGUESE DAY. In the image above, the UPEC band sets up before playing a concert for Portuguese Day at the Panama Pacific Exposition of 1915. The picture below shows an outside view of the Portuguese Pavilion. Before Portuguese Day, all the Portuguese fraternal societies participated in a parade on October 5, 1915, for Portuguese-American Day. According to Portuguese historian August Vaz, some of the parade's highlights included *A Portugueza*, the Portuguese National Hymn, with conductor Mario B. Camara and a choir of 100 girls, an address by representatives from California's governor and San Francisco's mayor, an English speech from Judge F. Mitchell, and a Portuguese speech from F. I. Lemos. Miss Carmelita and her choir of 100 girls regaled the crowd with the songs "I Love You California" and the "Star-Spangled Banner." Every Wednesday before the fair, the choir, made up of all interested Portuguese girls in the area over the age of 12, rehearsed under the direction of Mario B. Camara at the UPEC hall in San Leandro. (JAF and *Portuguese Immigrants*.)

EXHIBITION FUND-RAISER, HOTEL OAKLAND, 1914. The 1914 banquet at Hotel Oakland (pictured at left) was a fund-raiser for Dr. Sousa Bettencourt, J. A. Silveira, and F. I. Lemos's trip to Lisbon via Paris, to try to convince the Portuguese government to finance a Portuguese Pavillion at the Panama Pacific International Exhibition of 1915. Everyone believed it was a fool's mission. Nevertheless, upon their arrival in the President's Palace, the Portuguese president, senate, and house listened to their argument that a Portuguese Pavillion would glorify the Portuguese culture and be of long-lasting historic and commercial value. Their powers of persuasion worked: Portugal provided $125,000 to fund a pavillion honoring Portugal's colonial and maritime past, including Vasco da Gama's discovery of a searoute to India and Pedro Cabral's discovery of Brazil. It was a proud moment for Portugal and the 100,000 people of Portuguese descent living in California at the time. The pavillion itself was honored with 14 grand prizes, 35 medals of honor, 31 gold medals, 46 silver medals, 14 bronze medals, and one honorable mention. (Courtesy JAF and August Vaz.)

1930 UPEC CONVENTION, SAN LEANDRO. Pres. Frank E. Pinheiro (Frank E. Pine) presides over the 1930 convention, which celebrated the 50th anniversary of the UPEC in San Leandro. Born in Faial in 1889, Pinheiro enrolled in the seminary, which was one of the few ways to get a good education in the Azores at the time. After immigrating to Boston, Massachusetts, in 1906 to work as a barber, Pinheiro moved to Oakland and opened his own cleaners. In 1932, after a few years of working as a manager at Mission Chapel Mortuary, Pinheiro (Pine) opened his own shop with three partners. The Hanrahan, Wadsworth, Pine, and Borba Mortuary was also known as East Lawn Chapel. Pinheiro became very active in the UPEC and also served as president of Cabrilho Club No. 11 of Alameda County. (JAF and *Portuguese Immigrants*.)

65

Two Conventions. Above Antonio Fonte poses at a UPEC convention in San Jose. Below the women's organization UPPEC holds its annual convention in Oakland in 1935. UPEC members were very fond of their founder and first supreme president, Antonio Fonte and, in 1910, established an education fund in his honor. UPEC's supreme council, including director J. B. Mendonça, secretary Lucio Martin, and treasurer J. G. Mattos, voted to fund a school with Portuguese instruction for second-generation Portuguese children born in the United States. In 1915, they realized their dream, opening a school in the old Iberico Hall on Hays Street, where Prof. Candido Nunes taught reading, writing, history, and Portuguese; at night, the school offered classes for adults. (*A Garden Grows in Eden* and *Portuguese Immigrants*.)

UPEC CONVENTION SANTA CRUZ, 1916. UPEC president Manuel Gregoria Azevedo presided over UPEC's 1916 convention in Santa Cruz. Azevedo, an immigrant from Sao Jorge, immigrated to California in 1891. Also in attendance at the Santa Cruz convention were Mario B. Camara and F. I. Lemos. Delegates delighted in the delicious delicacies of an open-air banquet for 600, served on the beach. (*Portuguese Immigrants.*)

UPPEC CONVENTION, SANTA CRUZ, 1917. Delegates from the San Leandro branch of UPPEC No. 6 attend a convention in Santa Cruz along with delegates from UPPEC No. 1 from Oakland. According to Portuguese historian August Vaz, in 1901, the UPPEC was established in Oakland to do charitable acts and provide burial help in times of illness to its members. In 1905, the society paid $4 per week in sick benefits if a member required a doctor's care. (JAF and August Vaz.)

U.P.E.C. BAND - MANUEL C. MEDEIROS, CONDUCTOR
PORTUGAL DAY - JUNE 16, 1940 - G.G.I.E. - TREASURE ISLAND
Moulin

MANUEL C. MEDEIROS, BAND LEADER. The UPEC band, founded in 1905, poses after playing a set at the Golden Gate International Exposition on Treasure Island. All the buildings in the background were built specifically for the exposition and have been torn down. Band leader Manuel Medeiros immigrated from San Miguel in 1903, arriving in Oakland and working at the cotton mill. Medeiros worked for a sugar refinery in San Francisco in 1910 and for Southern Pacific Railway in 1917 before joining the Oakland Fire Department. Medeiros's true passion was music. In 1930, he led Oakland's fireman and police band and played bass in UPEC's band, serving as its assistant director in 1926 before succeeding Mario Bettencourt da Camara as UPEC's bandleader in 1936. Meideros served as UPEC's bandleader until health concerns forced him to resign in 1966. (JAF.)

Five

HOME FRONT

A DAY AT THE FAIR. A Portuguese band from the Cabrilho Civic Club in front of San Francisco's Shell Building departs for a day at the fair. The Portuguese Pavilion at the 1939–1940 World's Fair on Treasure Island featured a model of the 12-foot monument to the Portuguese explorer Cabrilho at its entrance. The monument and the Portuguese fraternal expenses for the fair were funded through the League of Portuguese Fraternal Societies of California. After the fair, the real Cabrilho monument on display at the simultaneous World's Fair in New York was donated to Cabrilho National Monument Park in Point Loma, California. The World's Fair was billed as a great educational experience, an advertisement beckoned fairgoers: "Do not miss going to this modern University, where lies much knowledge of a practical value for you. Portuguese Day at the Golden Gate World's Fair, September 6, 1939." (*Portuguese Immigrants* and JAF.)

UNION SCHOOL, 1897. Among those identified are Marlin Nelson, John Miller, William Silva, Bill Le Bon, ? Duarte, and principal W. H. Langdon. Langdon taught primary school and became principal before serving on California's supreme court. (SLPLHPC#222.)

UNION SCHOOL CLASS, 1897. Identified class members include Andrew Nelson, Mary Murray, Maggie Gill, Peter Lawrence, Minnie Miller, Rose Miller, ? Mattews, ? Toffelmier, Jennie Santos, Tony Costa, and ? Comatcha. The principal on the far right is W. H. Langdon, and the teacher on the far left is Miss Gill. (SLPLHPC#280.)

LINCOLN SCHOOL CLASS, 1916. This picture includes Lillian Phillips, Hyacinth Gonsalves, Winifred Wagner, Josephine Silva, Virnie Amaral, Jack Avelar, Roy Gomes, Madeline Silva, Clara Cabral, Aurora Perry, May Sardine, Edward Costa, John Sarmento, Eddie Mello, William Quadros, Bruno Vecchiarelli, William Silva, and Henry Rivera. Many of these students had family members who died in the flu epidemic after the war. (SLPLHPC#2054.)

UNION SCHOOL, C. 1890. Teachers and schoolchildren pose for a picture at Union School. Many Portuguese immigrants from the Azores had only received a third-grade education. Educational opportunity was a big reason for immigration. Today the Portuguese continue to value education. According to Dolores Vieira, "You can have everything but if you lose your education you have nothing; the only thing you can leave your children is a good education." (SLPLHPC#40.)

LINCOLN SCHOOL GRADUATION DAY, 1917. Lincoln's graduating class proudly holds up the American flag. Listed from left to right are the following: (first row) James Lippi, unidentified, Arnold Johansen, Tony Mello, Eddie Roberts, Charles Peralta, and Henry Twilson; (second row) Cyrel Flores, unidentified, Doris Ram, unidentified, Isabel Rogers, Lavilla Schafer, unidentified, Eleanor Silva, Evelyn Forsythe, and Lorinda Rego; (third row) Clemente August, John Gomez, Louis Lippi, unidentified, Tony Machado, unidentified, Olenda Silva, unidentified, Vera Edwards, Esther Hayes, and Dorthy Larson. Included in the fourth row in no particular order are Eddie Fretas, William Agrella, William Frank, Grace Steward, Ruby Best, and ? Peters. (SLPLHPC#119.)

LINCOLN SCHOOL PORTRAIT, C. 1920. Aurora Perry (Springer), who was very active in San Leandro Hospital, identified the following students: Sopia Dias is in the front row, third from the left; Mary Bettencourt is in the first row, fifth from the left, and Lois Arnold is in the front row, seventh from the left. (SLPLHPC#142.)

SAN LEANDRO ELEMENTARY, C. 1900. The members of the class are, from left to right, as follows: (first row) Margaret Peralta, unidentified, Aurora Perry, Ida Terra, unidentified, Hyacinth Gonsalves, and six unidentified children; (second row) unidentified, Beatrice Furtado, three unidentified children, Lois Arnald, Winifred Wagner, two unidentified children, John Pedro, and unidentified; (third row) Vernie Amaral, William Quadros, Henry Vieira, Bruno Vicarelli, William Silva, John Sarmento, Ernest Bettencourt, unidentified, Eddie Silva, Roy Silva, and unidentified. (Carlos Almeida.)

LINCOLN SCHOOL. This picture is not dated but it is probably from the early 1920s based on the girls' short hair cuts and clothing. Pictured from left to right are the following: (first row) Edgar Hages, Macrea Young, Sadie Lopez, Minnie Diaz, Ludovina Enos, Mary Paiva, Madeline Phillips, and Mabel Boga; (second row) Catherine Fleenor, Gertrude Thierry, Irene Bento, Eddie Catone, Donald Krampeter, Gerald Barker, and Lavoy Landis; (third row) Artie Bowan, Edward Thierry, Salvadore Williams, Marian Adams, Lillian Valance, Eliza Martinez, Francis Flewelling, and Mary Martin; (fourth row) Carolyn Nisbet, Frances Harper, Carmen Carlson, Violet Conway, teacher Arnold Davidson, Frank Bricker, David Wilson, Cecelia Silveira, and Roberta Young; (fifth row) Adeline Schorling, Reed Goodpasture, Dorothy Bissel, Dorothy Wickman, Lawrence Roberts, Irene Cabeceiras, Clarence Phillipa, Nelda Palmer, Fernando Affonso, and Anthony Mesa. (SLPLHPC#307.)

LINCOLN SCHOOL, CHRISTMAS DAY 1911. On a chalkboard in front of the class is a small sign that reads, "San Leandro X-mas, 1911." Those identified by the Moreira family include Florence Jones somewhere in the first row, Rhoda Perry in the second, Caroline Braga in the third, and Lucille August in the fifth. (SLPLHPC#1910.)

LINCOLN SCHOOL CLASS, C. 1908. Those identified by Mabel Garcia and Raymond Fraga are Edward Fraga, somewhere in the group in the lower left corner; John Costa somewhere in the first row on the steps; Reginald Wallace, in the second row, fourth from the left; Art Larsen in the third row, far left; Mable Garcia, location unknown; and May (Mary?) Pedro and Bill Cabole, somewhere in the third and fourth rows. (SLPLHPC#2162.)

UNION SCHOOL STUDENTS, 1893. Those identified include the teacher, Miss Whelan, in the back row, and Mr. Chapman, also in the back row on the right. In 1911, a U.S. Immigration sample of San Leandro's Portuguese residents found that second-generation Portuguese immigrant students had literacy rates of 100 percent in contrast to the 50 percent literacy rates of their parents, largely due to the fact a third-grade education was the standard in the Azores. Consequently many Portuguese immigrant parents placed a high value on education. (SLPLHPC#301.)

UNION SCHOOL CLASS OF 1897. Those identified include Stella Nelson, Mary Perry, Rose Marks, Rose Enos, Peggie Garcia, Minnie Cardoza, ? Halverson, principal W. H. Landgon (far right, fifth row), and class teacher, Miss Gleason (far left, fourth row). According to Portuguese historian Carlos Almeida, in 1895, Joao Pereira, a former whaler from Faial, worked as old Union School's custodian. (SLPLHPC#1561.)

ST. MARY'S SCHOOL PLAY. This 1897 picture at St. Mary's convent shows the students of St. Mary's dressed for their end-of-term school play. Identified students, from left to right, include Evelyn Kane, Carrie Silva, Emma Williams, Birdie Driver, Orallia Duarte, Madge McCarthy (angel), Mary Kane (Madonna), Isabel Focha (large angel), Bernice Calhoun (littlest angel), Emma Rose (angel), Salina Peralta, Rose Morris, Margaret Smiley (little kneeling angel), Aileen Dutra (at the well), and Louise Garcia (with harp). (SLPLHPC#1925 and Rosaline B. Correra.)

MABEL FURTADO'S BIRTHDAY PARTY. Mabel Furtado's family and friends gather in front of her house in San Leandro for a group portrait on her birthday. Miss Furtado's friends and family gathered again in 1910 to celebrate her reign as queen of San Leandro's cherry festival. (JAF.)

UNION SCHOOL CLASS OF 1909. Those pictured in the first row are unidentified. Included in the second row are Juanita Revekes, Rose Faria Lopez (center), and Jesse Jones (Mrs. Harold Almond). In the top row, listed from left to right, are George Nelson; Guy Smith, principal; Charlotte Lynch, teacher; unidentified; and George Demont. (SLPLHPC#153.)

SAN LEANDRO GRAMMAR SCHOOL. This picture dated 1920 is more likely from 1917, given the patriotic flags. Included in the first row are James Lippi, Arnold Johansen, Tony Mello, Charles Peralta, and Henry Twilson. Included in the second row are Cyrel Flores, vice principal Guy Smith, Doris Ram, Charlotte Lynch, and Laura Esperanza. (SLPLHPC#151.)

WORLD WAR I LUNCHEON. This picture shows a luncheon served by Oakland's UPEC to soldiers returning home from World War I. Many Portuguese immigrants volunteered to fight in the World War I Coast Artillery Corps, including Manuel Perreira, an immigrant from Pico who volunteered for the service in 1916 and worked in San Francisco for Union Iron Works after the war. (*Portuguese Immigrants* and SLPLHPC#11.)

FOOD RATIONING, 1917. Pictured here are Fred Hirschman (left) and constable J. H. Gallet. The sign reads, "Save Food, 120 Million Allies Must Eat." Everyone pitched in to win the war. Young men enlisted in the armed services and fought abroad, and local Portuguese families gave generously to the war effort. (SLPLHPC#437.)

WORLD WAR I PRIVATE ANTHONY SILVA.
Anthony Silva was stationed at Camp
Kearny in August 1918. Pvt. Anthony Silva
dedicated this photograph "To my true
friend, P. J. Bright, from Private Anthony
Silva, One of Uncle Sam's Go Get 'Em Boys."
(SLPLHPC#1833.)

One of Uncles Sams:-
-go-get-em boys

27
at
Camp Kearny
Aug. 1918
To my true   friend
P.J. Bright
from Private Anthony Silva

WORLD WAR I RECEPTION. Estudillo House
held a 1919 reception for World War I
veterans in the gardens under the grape
arbor. According to Portuguese historian
August Vaz, after the war in 1917, America
was rapt in anti-German and anti-foreigner
sentiment, even renaming the hamburger
"liberty steak." In this era of anti-foreign
sentiment, the Portuguese fraternal society
Uniao Portuguesa Continental do Estado
da California (UPC) formed in Oakland to
unite immigrants from continental Portugal
and preserve and promote Portuguese
heritage. (August Vaz and SLPLHPC#499.)

WORLD'S FAIR, 1939–1940. Above is an aerial view of the Golden Gate International Exposition at Treasure Island. At left is a Caterpillar truck working to construct Treasure Island. The Treasure Island Exposition was part of a huge WPA project. It cost $3,719,800 to construct the fair's buildings and drive 10,000 piles of rock. The World's Fair of 1939 (Golden Gate International Exposition) commemorated the completion of the Golden Gate and Bay Bridges. There were many notable performers, including Judy Garland and Sally Rand with her feather dance. The fair's entrance featured a giant statue of the female sea goddess Pacifica by sculptor Ralph Stackpole. The fair's purpose was to attract visitors to the San Francisco Bay and celebrate the diversity of Pacific cultures. September 6, 1939, Portuguese Day at the fair, featured beautiful floats from Portuguese fraternal societies. Portuguese radio talents and journalists were also in attendance. (JAF.)

STAND OF PORTUGAL. The Portuguese Pavilion at the Golden Gate Exhibition was built entirely through community donations totaling $6,829.64. The exhibit featured Portuguese hostesses dressed in peasant costumes and a chart of Portuguese industries in California. Mary Simas was voted Portuguese Day's queen, winning 200,650 votes. Her maids were Frances Fortuna and Marie June Silveira. It is estimated that 25,000 Portuguese spectators visited the Golden Gate Exhibition, roughly 25 percent of the 100,000 people of Portuguese descent living in California at the time. (*Portuguese Immigrants*.)

PORTUGUESE DAY AT THE FAIR. Portuguese Day was conceived through the League of Portuguese Fraternals, a body formed in 1937 to represent the collective interests of the Portuguese fraternal societies. Their first task was to decide how to best represent Portugal at the Golden Gate Exhibition of 1939. (*Portuguese Immigrants*.)

SPRSI No. 6 Float. Members from Sociedade Portuguesa Rainha Santa Isabel (SPRSI) No. 6 from East Oakland enjoy a day at the World's Fair on Treasure Island. Many came to the fair to see the 280-acre garden with more than 4,000 trees, small trees, shrubs, tropical grasses, and acres upon acres of flowers. Nighttime visitors marveled at the Tower of the Sun and Court of the Moon lit with colored lights representing the beauty of Pacific shores. (JAF.)

APPB Float. Pictured in 1939 is the Associacao Portuguesa Protectora e Beneficente (APPB) World's Fair float. APPB was formed in San Francisco in 1868. Portuguese historian August Vaz describes the society's aim to "*proteger os vivos e entrarrar os mortos* (protect the living and bury the dead)." Dr. Jose Bettencourt, San Francisco's vice consul of Portugal, was an early member, joining in 1877. In 1957, APPB merged with another fraternal, UPC, forming the United National Life Insurance Society. (August Vaz and JAF.)

UPPEC FLOAT.
Members from UPPEC No. 23 enjoy a day at the fair aboard their float, which reads, "God Bless America" and "Portugal: Jardim de Europa A Beira Mar Plantado," meaning "Portugal: Garden of Europe by the Sea." The float also features a world map, which shows the location of the United States and Portugal with the Azores Islands in the center, the point of origin for more than 80 percent of the Portuguese in California. (JAF.)

UPEC FLOAT. The UPEC World's Fair float features a woman in a traditional black head scarf worn in the Azores to symbolize a woman in mourning. According to Portuguese historian Carlos Almeida, UPEC's emblem (on the float's side) was originally designed by Jose Pimentel, who envisioned an insignia with "two flags, the Portuguese and the American, crossing each other; and a boat facing the sun, symbolizing Vasco da Gama in his trip to India." (JAF and *Portuguese Immigrants.*)

WAR AT HOME AND ABROAD. An advertisement from the March 1943 issue of *Fortune* magazine encourages Americans to act as rumor wardens to win the war. The below photograph shows a reunion of World War II soldiers in 1946. Included are George Castro, Johnnie Costa, Frankie Galvan, Tony Vigallon, Mike Luciano, Anthony Sanchez Jr., and Joe Moreno. Third from the right in the first row is Mike Castro. During the war, San Leandro's Portuguese sold war bonds, rationed supplies, and raised money to purchase artillery. According to Pacific Bridge Company's December 1, 1943, edition of their internal magazine, *The Bridge*, Alameda's Pacific Bridge Company employed many Bay Area Portuguese, including Joe Rodrick of Oakland and ship builder Ernie Vargas of Livermore. Top ship builders such as Joe Rodrick made $47 for 48 hours of work. According to Susan Vargas, Ernie Vargas drove to work by motorcycle. In March 1942, Vargas's motorcycle skidded on milk spilled by a milk truck, and he fell into a brief coma. After that, his wife made him give up the motorcycle for good. (*Fortune* magazine, Susan Vargas, SLPLHPC#42.)

GUN PURCHASED BY FRATERNAL
SOCIETIES. In 1941, the League of
Portuguese Fraternal Societies raised
$10,680.24 to donate two millimeter anti-
aircraft guns to the war effort. They are
pictured here in 1942 at Hotel Oakland.
Formed in 1937, the Portuguese League
of Fraternal Societies represented the
collective interests of all the fraternals.
Prior to pooling their resources to
purchase ammunition, the *liga* worked
together to plan Portuguese Day during
the Golden Gate Exposition. (JAF and
Portuguese Immigrants.)

BASIC TRAINING. Mac Moitozo took
his basic training at Fort Bliss, Texas, in
the Coast Guard Artillery. Moitozo sent
this picture home to his father, Manuel
Moitozo Sr. in San Jose, who took care
of the Okuba family's ranch near River
Oaks in San Jose when they were interned
during World War II. (Mac Moitozo.)

DR. JOAQUIM R. S. LEITE. In 1925, Leite spearheaded a petition to honor the Portuguese explorer Vasco Da Gama by renaming First Avenue (now Marina Boulevard) in San Leandro Vasco Avenue. The petition was temporarily successful and, in 1925, San Leandro became the first city in the nation to honor the explorer who discovered a new trade route to India and explored the Cape of Tormentas, which, after his exploration, was coined the Cape of Good Hope. Gama's journey is recounted in the epic poem *Lusiadas* by the Portuguese poet Camoes. Dr. Leite served also in 1925 as a Portuguese consulate representative in San Leandro. Dr. Leite's interest in cultural and civic affairs led him to teach a weekly Portuguese class to San Leandro businessmen through University of California. In his spare time, he used his military expertise gathered while working as a captain in the Portuguese army reserve to help the California branch of the National Guard allocated to San Leandro, Company F, 159th Infantry Division. (JAF.)

Six

COMMUNITY BUILDING

WORLD'S FAIR, 1939. Pictured here from left to right are L. J. Freeman; Harold Brayton, greeter; L. E. Bontz, member of California Commission; and Helen Lawrence, councilwoman from San Leandro, who was named "Mayor for a Day" at the World's Fair on Treasure Island. Helen Lawrence was born in Faial, Azores, and immigrated to the United States with her parents. After graduating from San Jose State College for Teachers, she taught at Lincoln School in San Leandro. Lawrence served 13 years on the city council before becoming mayor in 1941. During her term as mayor she made many civic improvements, including relocating city hall, creating new streets, and easing the flow of traffic around town. Lawrence was a pioneering woman: she was the first woman mayor in San Leandro, from 1941 to 1943, and America's first Portuguese mayor. Her husband George was a wholesale distributor for Carnation Milk Products. (SLPLHPC#872 and *Portuguese Immigrants*.)

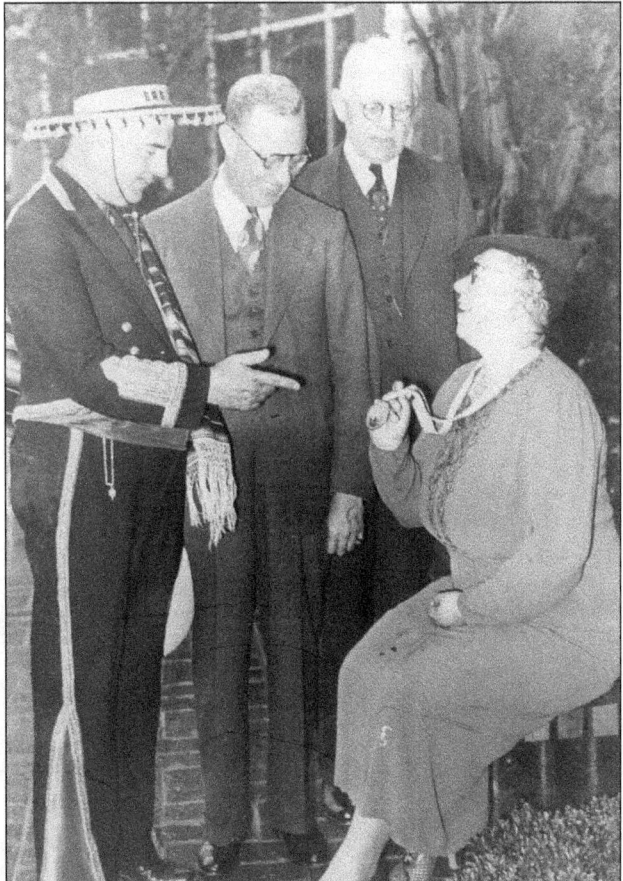

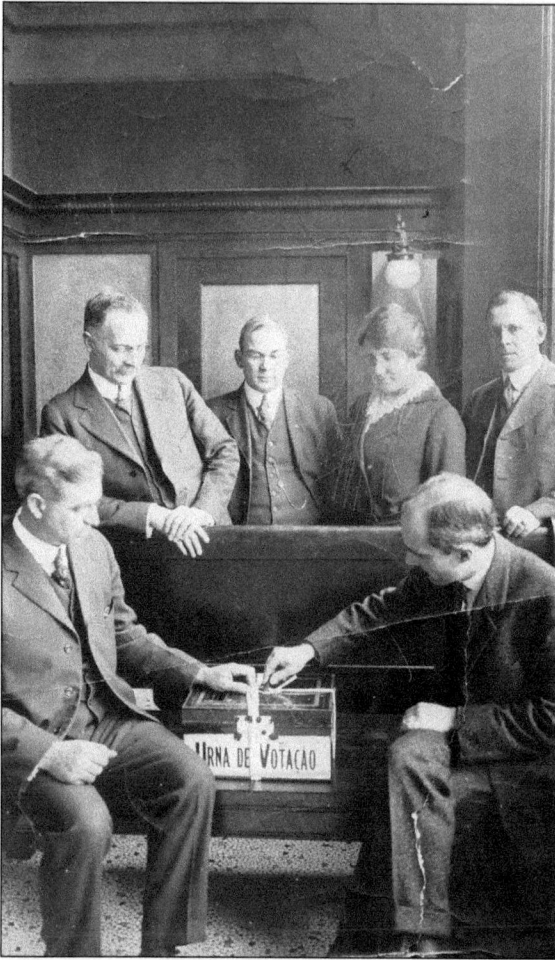

PORTUGUESE AMERICAN BANK IN SAN FRANCISCO. The photograph at left captures the election of the bank's officers. Pictured by the ballot box are president Joaquim Silveira (right) and vice president John Enas. Standing from left to right are cashier V. Figueiredo, and directors J. B. Mendonça, Ana Silveira, and A. Henas. Joaquim S. Silveira succeeded M. T. Freitas as the bank's president. Freitas, an immigrant from San Jorge Island in the Azores, founded the Portuguese American Bank of San Francisco in 1905, serving as its president until 1912. Freitas had worked his way up: he started out as a busboy in San Francisco, then became a successful restaurateur, and was finally able to purchase the Home Ranch in San Rafael and other holdings in Marin County. In addition to the San Francisco branch, the Portuguese American Bank had branches in Los Banos, Oakland, and Newman. The bank was quite successful; especially popular were its safety deposit boxes, renting for $2.50 a year. The Oakland branch alone had nearly $3 million in assets as of 1915. Below center, in a 1912 photograph of the cherry festival, is the bank of San Leandro, whose directors included J. B. Mendonça. (Carlos Almeida and SLPLHPC#939.)

BOND SIGNING, 1938. Pictured above signing city bonds for 185,000 are, from left to right, L. J. Freeman, chamber manager; Art Silva, city treasurer; Ed Hutchings, city clerk; and Earl Derry, mayor (in chair). Silva worked with city councilwoman Helen Lawrence, who became San Leandro's first female mayor and the first Portuguese mayor in America. (SLPLHPC#860.)

BREAKING GROUND AT FRIDEN. In the picture at right, the Friden Calculating Machine Company breaks ground at Washington Avenue on June 2, 1936. From left to right are Gertrude Perry, Carl Friden, and police chief J. F. Peralta. William Silva, who attended San Leandro elementary school with Aurora Perry (Springer), was a member of the UPEC and worked for the Friden Calculating Machine Company, which later was purchased by the Singer Corporation. (SLPLHPC#1193.)

LIGHTHOUSE SURROUNDED BY SMOKE. At left, a lighthouse is engulfed in plumes of smoke as the volcano Capelinhos off the island of Faial erupts. Ashes made fields and houses uninhabitable for years. Villagers didn't have the money to rebuild or excavate their homes; many took advantage of Kennedy's special visa for 1,500 families affected by the volcano. (Antonio Furtado.)

THE VOLCANO CAPELINHOS, FAIAL, 1957. Above, Antonio Furtado's map shows the location of Capelinhos off the island of Faial. The picture below dramatically illustrates the extent of the volcano's destruction as villagers, homeless because of the eruption, sort through the rubble. (Antonio Furtado.)

RESOLUTION NO. 3

WHEREAS, the Kennedy and Pastore Relief Bill providing for the admission of 1500 homeless persons from the Island of Faial, Azores, has been duly approved by the Senate of the United States and to become law requires only the approval of the House of Representatives;

WHEREAS, the admission of the 1500 persons from Faial contemplated by said bill would be an act of mercy and in keeping with the traditions of the United States, in receiving within its borders people who through no fault of theirs became displaced or homeless;

WHEREAS, the homeless of Faial Island have blood ties with a large segment of the population of the United States who were born or are the descendants of people from Faial, who by their outstanding qualities of character have proven to be an asset to our country and the communities where they reside;

WHEREAS, the membership of the Luso-American Fraternal Federation believes that the admission of the 1500 homeless persons contemplated under the Kennedy and Pastore Relief Bill would be for the best interest of the United States, and would strengthen the ties of friendship that bind the people of the Azores Island to the people of this country;

NOW, THEREFORE, BE IT RESOLVED, that the assembly of the Luso-American Fraternal Federation, representing 14,000 California families from every part of the State, assembled in convention at San Jose, California, go on record as indorsing the said Kennedy and Pastore Bill, and that a telegram be sent to all the California representatives in the Congress of the United States, urging upon them the approval of said bill.

KNOW ALL MEN BY THESE PRESENTS, that the undersigned, Secretary of the United National Life Insurance Society, and ex-officio State Secretary of the Luso-American Fraternal Federation, California State Council of the United National Life Insurance Society, does hereby certify that the foregoing resolution was unanimously adopted at the Annual State Convention of the Luso-American Fraternal Federation in San Jose, California, on August 19, 1958.

WITNESS my hand and seal of the Corporation this 22nd day of August, 1958.

Jack Costa
Secretary

AZOREAN RELIEF ACT. On August 18, 1958, the Luso American Fraternal Federation approved a resolution calling for the support of California congressmen for an Azorean relief act (left). Following the eruption of Capelinhos in 1957, the U.S. Congress under the leadership of Sen. John F. Kennedy of Massachusetts and Sen. John Pastore of Rhode Island passed a relief act allowing 1,500 families from Faial who were victims of the volcano to immigrate to the New World. Thousands of new Azorean immigrants were called and sponsored by their families in America after this relief act. Below is a Western Union Telegram, which shows the passage of a resolution in 1958 that allowed 1,500 families from Faial made homeless by the volcano to come to America. (JAF and Antonio Furtado.)

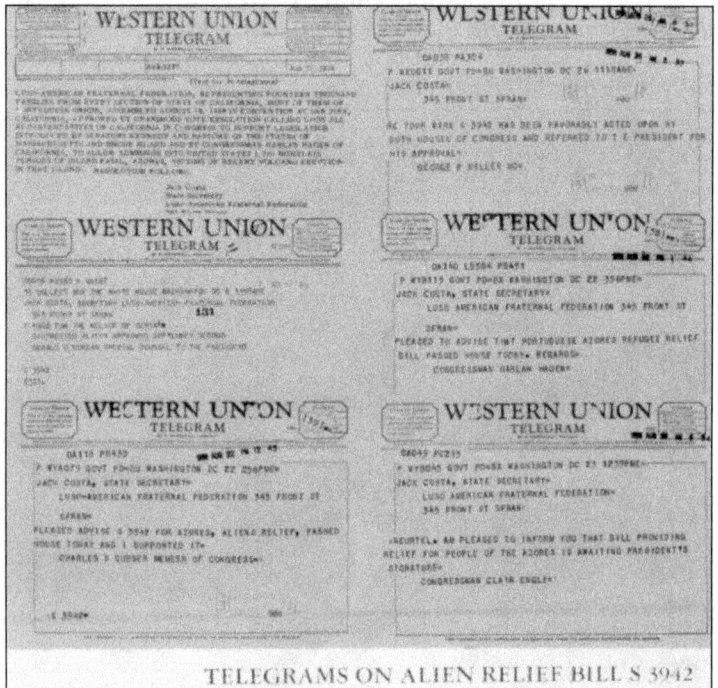

TELEGRAMS ON ALIEN RELIEF BILL S 3942

EMIGRATION BUREAU, SAN MIGUEL, 1957. Carlos Almeida (left) worked as personnel manager for the Canadian National Railway. Emigrants' hands were checked for calluses to see if they had done any hard labor, such as masonry, carpentry, or farm work. Merchants hammered their hands, salesmen and cashiers put dirt on them. Emigrants contracting with Canadian Railway were not allowed to come to Canada if they had ever applied for a U.S. visa. As a Portuguese emigration officer in Ponta Delgada from 1953 to 1956, Almeida received mainly three emigration requests: for the United States, Brazil, and Canada. For 200 years, Azoreans shipped out to parts unknown. Now the tides have shifted: the Azores are a destination, not a point of departure. According to Almeida, people return to the Azores because of the quiet lifestyle with "just the sea and a tight-knit community." Below Portuguese cinematographer Antonio Furtado's 1957 map shows the Azorean archipelago in relation to America and Europe. (*Acores e o Vulcao dos Capelinhos* by Antonio Furtado and *Portuguese Immigrants*.)

DR RAMIRO DUTRA. Born in Ponta Delgada, San Leandro's sister city in the Azores, Ramiro Dutra came to San Leandro as a student and lived with his aunt Maria Ascençao Rogers, later attending University of California–Berkeley and University of California–Davis. Dutra served in the navy, where he received many distinguished citations. Dutra also received the Order of Santiago from the Portuguese government. After receiving a Ph.D. in biochemistry, he became a distinguished professor of nutrition and food technology at the Technical University of the State of California. (Carlos Almeida.)

ST. ANTHONY'S HOSPITAL. In 1904, St. Anthony's Hospital in Oakland was the first Portuguese hospital in America. Dr. M. M. Enos, Joaquim A. Silveira, J. J. Bettencourt, Alexandre Borges, Joao Balra, Jose D. Oliveira, and David Williams formed the Portuguese Hospital Association, which was run entirely in Portuguese, to serve the needs of the community. Enos also served as director of San Francisco's Portuguese American Bank. (*Portuguese Immigrants.*)

MUSICAL LEGACY. Congressman Tony Coelho and Philip Sousa III pose on the steps of the U.S. Capitol. Coelho was proud to stand with the grandson of John Philip Souza, composer of America's national march. (JAF.)

SOUZA AND HIS BAND. Pictured here with his band is John Philip Souza, a prolific composer of Portuguese descent who wrote the march of the United States, "Stars and Stripes Forever," in 1896, and conducted the UPEC band at the Panama Pacific Exhibition of 1915. (JAF.)

MARIO'S SHOESHINE. Mario Polvorosa built his shoeshine business (below) next to the Portuguese UPEC home office (above). In the far right (below) is the cornerstone of the UPEC building. Polvorosa was a city councilman during the 1970s. In the front center of the store, he kept pictures of his famous customers, including politicians, sports figures, and Admiral Nimitz. A block from city hall, Polvorosa's shop became a hub for the city's politicians. (Carlos Almeida.)

UPEC NEW HOME OFFICE, 1964. The picture above, taken December 12, 1964, shows the ribbon-cutting ceremony for the new UPEC office located at East Fourteenth and Chumalia Streets. UPEC's entire membership donated to fund the new building, a construction project that took more than a year to complete. The women and men in the back rows are unidentified; behind the ribbon in the first row are, from left to right, Vincent Azevedo; the gentleman in the hat is Jack Peixoto; with his hand on the shear is Dr. Manuel P. Silva, consul general of Portugal; and holding the scissors is Jack D. Maltester, San Leandro's mayor at the time. Holding the handles is Manuel Silva, supreme president of the UPEC, next to him is Dr. Luiz J. Madeira, and behind him in the dark suit stands Joseph A. Freitas. The UPEC office is visible below on the far left. (Nello Gianini and JAF.)

J. A. Freitas Library, 1972. The mannequin in back is dressed in the typical robe worn by members joining the UPEC during initiation ceremonies in the late 1880s. Some founding members of the UPEC from mainland Portugal and the Azores were masons. Today the library houses three major collections: English works about Portugal and the Portuguese, the history of the Azores, and the history of Portugal. (JAF.)

Girl Scouts visit the J. A. Freitas Library. Here Girl Scouts visit the UPEC library. Located in the UPEC Cultural Center at 1120 East Fourteenth Street in San Leandro, the J. A. Freitas Library holds more than 11,000 Portuguese-related titles, including periodicals dating back to the 1880s. Directly across from the library is a wonderful museum with artifacts showcasing the Portuguese contribution to the community since the 1880s. Both the library and museum are open Monday through Friday from 9 a.m. to 4:30 p.m. (JAF.)

WIK-I-SH-TA CAMP FIRE GROUP. The group that visited the library that day included Ill Randall, Carole Harrington, Sheri Souza, Linda Titus, Debra Beuelna, Linda Service, Jacqui Watson, Nancy Hesseltine, Beth Baronian, Ann Reed, Mrs. Dale Reed, leader Mrs. Robert Baronian, and Mrs. Jack E. Watson. During their visit to the J. A. Freitas Library, the campfire girls admired the artifacts of the UPEC. (JAF.)

J. A. FREITAS LIBRARY, 1970. Maria Pachao wears a Minho dress from Northern Portugal. The J. A. Freitas Library was founded as a research center for individuals interested in the Portuguese. The library includes books donated from individuals and institutions, including the Gulbenkian Foundation; House of Bragança; Dr. Manuel Pedro Ribeiro da Silva, consul of Portugal; and cultural institutes in Ponta Delgada, Horta, Angra do Heroismo, and Funchal. In addition to its many books, the library boasts historical photographs, sheet and recorded music, and microfilm of Portuguese newspapers published in California. (JAF.)

1880 — U.P.E.C. Centennial Executive Committee — 1980

Maria L. Fialho
Souvenirs

Telmo Fialho
Reception — Decorations

Jose Goulart
Old Timer's Ball

Maria Goulart
Grand Ball

Hortense Mendes
Queen's Ball

Luis Mendes
Special Arrangements

Maria C. Rezendes
Sightseeing

Marie Xavier
Visitor's Reception

Tony Xavier
Parade

UPEC CENTENNIAL COMMITTEE. Here pictured are nine members of UPEC's 1980 Centennial Committee. Listed from top to bottom, left to right are: Maria L. Fialho, souvenirs; Telmo Fialho, reception and decorations; Jose Goulart, old timer's ball; Maria Goulart, grand ball; Hortense Mendes, queen's ball; Luis Mendes, special arrangements; Maria C. Rezendes, sightseeing; Marie Xavier, visitor's reception; and Tony Xavier, parade. Tony Xavier joined the UPEC in 1963 and served as the secretary for the Holy Ghost Association of Alvarado Street. In 1982, Tony Xavier, the secretary-treasurer of San Leandro's Irmandade Do Divino Espirito Santo (IDES) of Alvarado Street, served as chairman of the Holy Ghost Association of Alvarado Street's centennial celebration. San Leandro's mayor Valance Gill proclaimed May 28, 29, and 30, in 1982 as Portuguese Week to honor 100 years of Holy Ghost Festas in San Leandro. (CACSAIDES.)

1880 — U.P.E.C. Centennial Executive Committee — 1980

Carlos Almeida
Chairman

Dr. Luis J. Madeira
Vice-Chairman

Peggy Hannigan Collett
Secretary

John Botelho
Treasurer

Maria F. Almeida
Registration

John H. Alves
Mass and Luncheon

Antone E. Braga
Pioneer Dinner

Felicissimo Carvalheira
Exhibition

Eddie Costa
Installation

CENTENNIAL COMMITTEE. Posing in old-time regalia are nine members of UPEC's centennial executive committee, including (top to bottom, left to right) Carlos Almeida, chairman; Dr. Luiz J. Madeira, vice chairman; Peggy Hannigan Collett, secretary; John Botelho, treasurer; Maria F. Almeida, registration; John H. Alves, mass and luncheon; Antone E. Braga, pioneer dinner; Felicissimo Carvalheira, exhibition; and Eddie Costa, installation. Centennial executive committee chairman Carlos Almeida, born in San Miguel in 1933, worked as an emigration officer in Ponta Delgada in 1951 before settling in San Leandro in 1958, where he served as UPEC's secretary-treasurer for 36 years. Almeida's civic activities included serving as president of San Leandro's Historical-Cultural Commission (1973), president of the library board of trustees (1974), coordinator for the Portuguese Immigrant Monument (1964), founder of the J. A. Freitas Library (1965), and president of the League of Portuguese Fraternal Societies (1981). Personally invited to the White House by Reagan, Carter, and Johnson, Almeida was also decorated with the Order of Prince Henry by the Portuguese government in 1980. (*Portuguese Immigrants.*)

SAN LEANDRO BICENTENNIAL, 1972. Identified in this image are Maria Fagundes, third from left, and Debbie and Patty Almeida in the back far right. Maria Almeida is in front on the right with John Botelho. Parade attendants included members of the Portuguese fraternal societies IDES, UPEC, UPPEC, SPRSI, APUMEC (a fraternal society for the Island of Madeira), and the SES. The float featured dairy farming and agricultural motifs incorporated with elements from traditional Azorean pastimes to represent the rich cultural heritage of San Leandro's Portuguese community. This float was constructed by all of the Portuguese fraternals in San Leandro to celebrate San Leandro's bicentennial. San Leandro's bicentennial committee helped preserve the town's cultural capital and was able to secure bronze California State historical markers for significant historical points of interest, including the oyster beds at Mulford Point and the monument to the Portuguese immigrant in Root Park. (*Portuguese Immigrants* and Nello Gianani.)

Seven

HOLY GHOST FESTA

HOLY GHOST PARADE, SAN LEANDRO PLAZA, 1933. Elsie Marshall is pictured here in the center wearing a crown. Her maids on either side are Marie Fagundes and Florence Cruz. In the background are Manuel Rogers, John Costa Silva, Manuel Garcia, and George Phillips. San Leandro's Holy Ghost Festa started in 1882 to celebrate the miracle of Queen Isabel, who made a *promessa* to the Holy Ghost in 1279 that she would give up her crown if the Holy Ghost sent a miracle to feed her people who were suffering through a terrible famine. When she left the church, ships laden with food entered Lisbon's harbor. Pope Urban VIII canonized St. Isabel in 1625. Each year, the IDES of Alvarado Street honored St. Isabel's memory with a Holy Ghost Festa spanning two days, starting with an introduction of the queen followed by singing, dancing, fireworks, and carnival. Sunday morning brought the crowning, the parade with the queen and her maids, and a high mass followed by *sopa* and *carne* (bread and meat) for everyone. (CACSAIDES.)

I.D.E.S. (HOLY GHOST-ESPIRITO SANTO) ALVARADO ST.

SAN LEANDRO, CA

HOLY GHOST INSIGNIA. Above is IDES of Alvarado Street's Holy Ghost Insignia. The original five founders of IDES of Alvarado Street were Charles Cross, Jose F. Focha, Jose B. Mendonça, and M. J. de Souza. Mendonça emigrated from Faial to San Francisco in 1868 through the Isthmus of Panama, leased more than 1,000 acres in the San Leandro foothills from Don Francisco Peralta, and in three years bought a 200-acre farm, becoming Thomas Mulford's partner in the Mulford Ranch. Mendonça also founded the San Leandro Mill and Lumber Company and served as a director of old First National Bank of San Leandro. Mendonça's greatest triumph came when he managed to purchase land along the shores of the marina, which reminded him of the windswept island of his birth. (CACSAIDES.)

PORTRAIT OF ST. ISABEL. In California, the Holy Ghost Festa honors St. Isabel who, in 1296, dedicated a festival to honor the Holy Ghost and to feed the poor. The queen of the festa is the human embodiment of this spirit of generosity, and her procession leads the crowd to a festival where food is free for all who wish to partake. (JAF.)

HOLY GHOST CHAPEL ON ALVARADO STREET. In 1882, Joseph Francis Focha spearheaded a drive to pool funds from San Leandro's Portuguese community to purchase a chapel and hall behind the Best Tractor Company. Focha was a carpenter and volunteered to build the Holy Ghost Chapel and Hall. The trees Focha planted long ago still provide shade for Holy Ghost Festa participants. Today a portrait of Focha and the articles of incorporation for the IDES of Alvarado Street are on display inside the chapel. (CACSAIDES.)

ST. LEANDER'S CATHOLIC CHURCH, 1957. At left is old St. Leander's Catholic Church on West Estudillo and Carpentier Streets. According to Carlos Almeida, in 1896, St. Leander's received $25 to hold the Holy Ghost Mass and bless the beef for the *sopas* and *carne*. The whole Portuguese community joined together to plan the Holy Ghost Festa, with each member donating what they could as thanks for the blessings of the Holy Ghost. (CACSAIDES.)

LOUISA DABNER FOCHA AND JOSEPH FRANCIS FOCHA. Joseph Francis Focha, first president of the IDES of Alvarado Street in San Leandro, was born January 5, 1844, on Flores, Azores. Focha was a whaler who jumped ship to settle in San Leandro, working for the Best Tractor and San Leandro Plow Company. The father of Joseph's wife, Louisa, was John Davina, who emigrated from Pico, working as a cook on a whaling ship. Settling in New Bedford, Massachusetts, a Portuguese settlement on the East Coast, Davina met and married his wife, Maria Jesus Machado. Like many Portuguese immigrants, Davina Americanized his name, taking the name Dabner. In 1856, the Dabners relocated to a farm on Haas Avenue in San Leandro and had three children, including Louisa Dabner, who married Joseph Francis Focha IDES of San Leandro. (CACSAIDES.)

ORIGINAL HOLY GHOST CROWN SAN LEANDRO. Around 1870, Maria Dabner held the first Holy Ghost celebrations in San Leandro at her house on Haas Avenue. Dabner made a Holy Ghost crown herself from wire and silk, adorning the crown with a ball representing the world, a cross representing Christ, and a dove symbolizing the Holy Ghost. The priest at St. Leander's blessed the crown and a scepter also adorned with a ball and dove. For several years, each Pentecost Sunday, the Dabners hosted the Holy Ghost celebration with a ceremony followed by *sopas* and *carne* for all. (CACSAIDES.)

EARLY HOLY GHOST FESTA. Queen Marie ? (center) carries the holy ghost crown. Also pictured are Mamie Enos, Rose Matoza, Mae Rogers, and Lena Phillips. Before the Holy Ghost Chapel was built, families would take turns hosting the Holy Ghost Festa in their homes. (CACSAIDES.)

FOCHA FAMILY HOME, 20 DABNER STREET, 1911. Pictured here from left to right are the following: (first row, standing) Anna Focha, Maud (Focha) Perry, Rosaline (Focha) Correia, Ida Bell Focha, Louisa (Dabner) Focha, Joseph Focha, and Mary (Focha) Vargas; (second row) John Focha with his wife Ida Focha. The two children in front are Harold Peary (left) and Gladys Correia. One of the Fochas grandchildren, Hal Peary, went on to become a radio and television star known as "the Great Gildersleeve." (CACSAIDES.)

ASHLAND HOLY GHOST, 1925. Pictured above is Ashland Holy Ghost queen and maids pose during neighboring San Lorenzo's Ashland Holy Ghost Festa of 1925. Queen Mabel Fields poses with maid Dorothy Silveira and rod girls Marie Xavier and Mary Silva. The 1926 picture below shows queen Mabel Fields with Marie Garcia (Xavier) in the foreground. The Holy Ghost queen and her maids marched in Holy Ghost parades throughout the state—a tradition that continues today. In return for the blessings of the Holy Ghost, members of the community came together volunteering their time and contributing funds for the celebration. For four generations, San Leandro's Xavier have volunteered their time to cook *sopas* and *carne*, marinate lupini, manage treasury funds, and organize the annual parades. The tradition of giving thanks for blessings harkens back to the traditional Azorean festas. spiritually connects Portuguese immigrants to the islands of their birth. (CACSAIDES.)

HOLY GHOST FESTA, 1906. Pictured at right is the Portuguese queen of the Holy Ghost Festa of the IDES of Alvarado Street getting ready to march in the 1906 parade. In the front row her royal court includes Theresa Santos and Ida Canton. Pictured below is a snapshot of the 1906 parade. According to Portuguese historian Carlos Almeida, at the turn of the century, San Leandro's festa was a devout religious ceremony that brought the whole community together. In 1886, under secretary Lucindo J. Martins, San Leandro's IDES brotherhood raised funds to pay for a Holy Ghost hall and a little chapel called an *imperio*. Portuguese immigrants decorated the corner of Antonio and Alvarado Streets with colored lights and flags like the ones they had in the Azores. The association's 1886 records show that IDES paid $18 for a cow, $2 for the baker to roast it, and $20 for a cascade of fireworks. (CACSAIDES.)

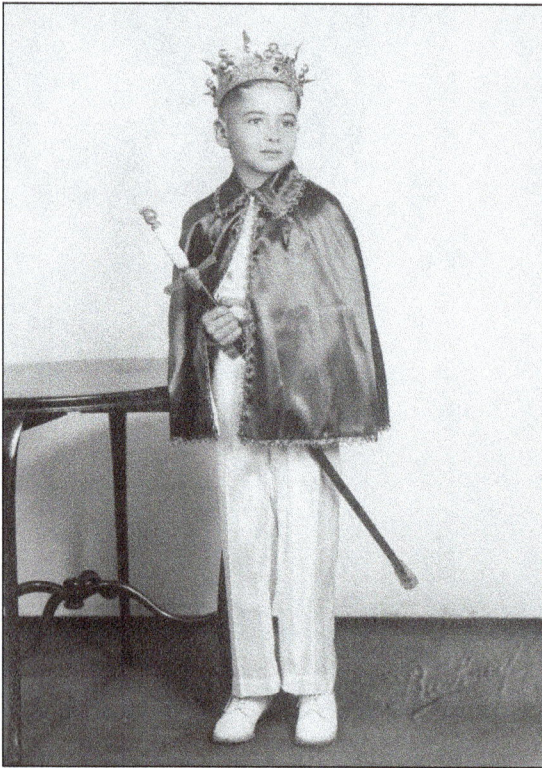

JULIO A. MARTINS. Pictured here as a child, Julio A. Martins was devout at a young age. Martins entered the priesthood and later became Monseigneur Martins with a parish in Hayward, where he presided over many Portuguese religious ceremonies, including baptisms and weddings. (JAF.)

UPPEC No. 6. The woman's organization UPPEC No. 6 marches in San Leandro's Holy Ghost Festa of 1918. Those identified in the drill team include Mary Faustino, third from the left, and Sadie Dutra, second from the left. (CACSAIDES.)

OAKLAND CHURCH GATHERING, EARLY 1930S. Pictured here is a procession of Oakland's Sociedade Maria SS Auxiliadora in the early 1930s. For Portuguese immigrants far from home, church activities provided a familiar environment and a social nucleus. In 1892, a new Catholic church, St. Joseph's Portuguese National Church, with services in Latin and Portuguese, opened in Oakland to serve the growing number of Portuguese parishioners in the area. (JAF Library and Alvin Graves, *Immigrants in Agriculture*.)

SPRSI FLOR DE UNIAO, 1913. The SPRSI drill team poses for a picture before a parade during their 1913 convention in San Leandro. Old St. Mary's School is in the background. The SPRSI (Sociedade Portuguesa Rainha Santa Isabel) was a woman's fraternal society. The SPRSI had dances, which were a source of social interaction, and provided an insurance policy in case of death. (August Vaz and SLPLHPC#40.)

SPRSI AND IDES CONVENTIONS. The Portuguese Society of Queen St. Isabel (Sociedade Portuguesa Rainha Santa Isabel— SPRSI) held its 26th annual convention July 12–15, 1926, in San Francisco. Many women from San Leandro attended. The SPRSI was founded in 1901. According to Portuguese historian August Vaz, the society grew out of a small group of 30 women who met in 1898 at Oakland's St. Joseph's Church to start a women's society with the motto, "Sociability and Protection." At right is an IDES convention.

SPRSI AND IDES CONVENTIONS. SPRSI's aim was to preserve Portuguese culture, language, and religion while supporting charitable endeavors. By 1928, SPRSI's charity fund had grown to $46,000 and death benefits totaled more than $4 million. SPRSI was known for its charitable works, including establishing a scholarship fund for high school seniors in the 1950s. SPRSI membership during the 1960s included 158 councils throughout the state with a membership of almost 14,000. Below is an IDES convention. (JAF and August Vaz, *The Portuguese in California*.)

FESTA QUEENS. Past Holy Ghost Festa queens Georgina Silveira and Mary Garcia Xavier take a break posing on their old-fashioned car about 1935. Leonora Silveira was queen in 1913. The president of the Holy Ghost Association of Alvarado Street in 1913 was Joaquin Ignacio da Silva. (JAF.)

OAKLAND BASEBALL TEAM. Portuguese boys from San Leandro often went to neighboring Oakland to watch the Oakland baseball team. Portuguese ball players participated in games throughout the Bay Area, including Calvin Silva, Wilbur Borba, and Miguel Perry, who played at the San Leandro's Thrasher Athletic Club in 1927. (JAF.)

114

Eight

ARTS AND RECREATION

BALL GAME IN SAN FRANCISCO, 1922. Frank Bettencourt of San Leandro was a ball player and also a famous musician. His band, Frank's Orchestra, used to play the Houston, Texas, oil clubs. (JAF.)

FESTIVAL OF NATIONS. California's Festival of Nations was held at the Oakland Auditorium and put on by the International Institute. The festival celebrated California's diversity, boasting a cast of "1,000 new Americans." The festival took place on Halloween, and many Portuguese from San Leandro traveled to Oakland for the event. (JAF.)

FESTIVAL OF NATIONS PERFORMERS. Maria A Rogers (left), George Pimentel (center), and Batista ? Jr. pose for a picture in the Oakland Auditorium at the Festival of Nations. Maria Rogers and George Pimentel were both instrumental in getting a statue dedicated to Portuguese immigrants in Root Park. Rogers was the person who expressed her dismay to Carlos Almeida at not being able to find anyone on the West or East Coasts interested in the project, and Pimentel served as chairman of the special events committee of San Leandro's chamber of commerce, working closely with the UPEC to coordinate the monument's dedication ceremony in Root Park. (*Portuguese Immigrants.*)

UPEC BAND, 1915. Above, Portuguese musicians play an impromptu party in San Leandro. Below is UPEC's band of 1915. Behind the man with the drum mallet and holding the clarinet stands Joe Freitas. First on the left standing with the bass is Manuel Medeiros. The UPEC band played many concerts throughout the state. Manuel Medeiros was the future conductor of the UPEC band and played at the World's Fair on Treasure Island in 1940. (JAF.)

PEDRO L. C. SILVEIRA, OWNER, JORNAL PORTUGUES. At left is a portrait of Pedro Silveira, the owner of *Jornal Portugues*. Below left is a snapshot of the outside of *Jornal Portugues* on East Fourteenth Street in Oakland. In 1886, Silveira emigrated from Flores, Azores, at the age of 15. After working in the Northern California mines, he married Maria Nunes. He worked for several Portuguese newspapers including *A Liberdade* in 1907 and the *Uniao*. In 1917, he bought *O Arauto*. In 1932, Silveira took control of *Jornal Portugues*, which formed from the merger of three papers—*Imparcial*, *Jornal de Noticias*, and *Colonia Portuguesa*. Silveira's leadership made the Oakland paper thrive. In 1938, President Roosevelt wrote to the *Jornal Portugues* commending it on its 50th year of excellent publishing. The Oakland-based paper helped educate immigrants about their ancestry and kept them up to date about the news from all the Portuguese *colonias* in America and the greater Portuguese-speaking world abroad. (August Vaz, *The Portuguese in California*, and JAF.)

PRINTING PRESS AND ARMANDO AGUIAR. Pictured above is Alberto Correa, the Linotypist seated in the center amidst the *Jornal Portugues* printing press. The image at right shows Portuguese journalist Armando Aguiar at his writing desk. According to Portuguese historian August Vaz, in 1927, Oakland was known as the center of the Portuguese press in America. Like the Portuguese fraternal societies, the Portuguese press helped immigrants in the *colonia* preserve their ties with their native culture in the New World. The newspaper also served an educational purpose, as literate immigrants would often read to those who could neither read nor write, thus enabling them to learn about the news of the day. (August Vaz, *The Portuguese in California*, and JAF.)

NATURALIZATION CERTIFICATE AND INSPECTION CARD. Above is Albert Correa's naturalization certificate. Below is Correa's inspection card, which he had to fill out upon entry to the United States. Albert Correa was editor of Oakland's *Jornal Portugues* for many years. Correa had a vast library and donated many Portuguese books to the J. A. Freitas Library in San Leandro when it was just beginning in the 1960s. Correa's daughter Aurielia Correa married Lewis Correia of New Bedford, Massachusetts. Albert Correa's son-in-law, Lewis Correia, was born on the Cape of Good Hope in South Africa in 1916, immigrating with his father Anibal Correia to Madeira in 1919 and to America around 1936. After working as a painter, in 1938, Lewis Correia went to work at University of California–San Francisco's physical plant. Correia was very involved in charitable causes and, in 1939, he raised funds to send to flood victims in Madeira. Correia also served his country in the navy, fighting against the Axis powers during World War II. (*Portuguese Immigrants* and JAF.)

ALBERT CORREA, EDITOR *JORNAL PORTUGUES*. To the right is a portrait of Albert Correa, and below is his vaccination card. Albert Correa emigrated from Lisbon, Portugal, arriving September 1919 in New Bedford, Massachusetts, before moving to Oakland to work as an editor at *Jornal Portugues*. At the turn of the century, one of the most notable papers was M. B. Camara's newspaper, *A Chronica*. Camara defended the Portuguese culture against a *San Francisco Chronicle* article dated November 14, 1895, which questioned the means Portuguese used to get their land in Africa and suggested that the Portuguese community was involved with the prostitution and promiscuity of young girls. In a time when anti-immigration sentiment was rampant, Camara's article, "A Lesson in History to Some of the San Franciscan Journalists," dated December 20, 1895, shed light on Portugal's noble and glorious past, and refused to tolerate ignorant and libelous accusations "directed at not only the Portuguese mothers resident in San Francisco, but all of that nationality in general." (JAF.)

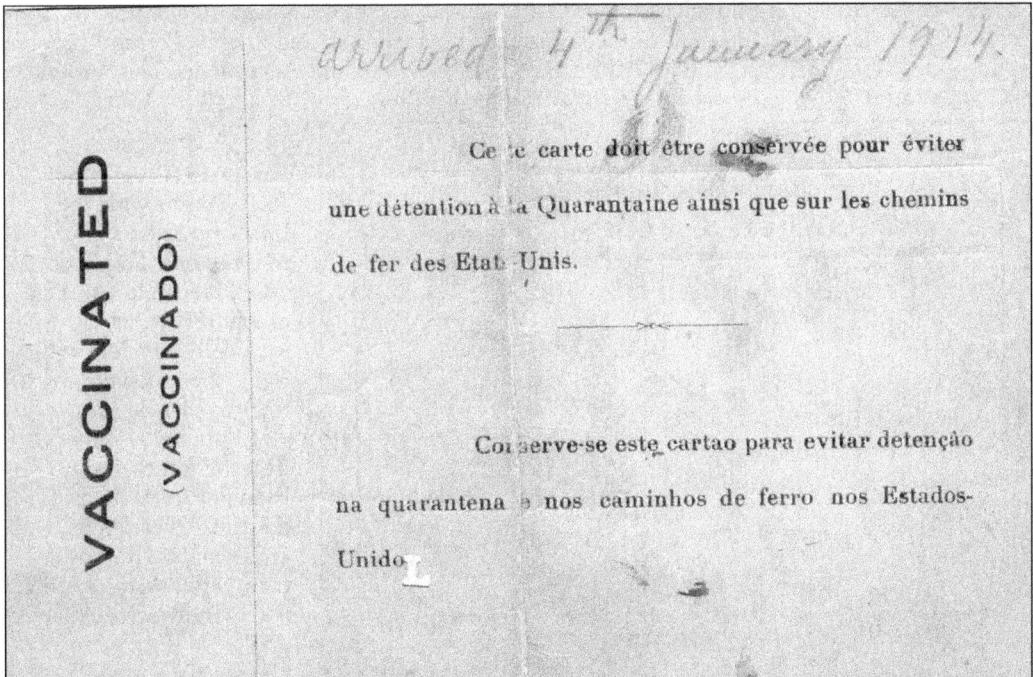

arrived 4th January 1914.

VACCINATED
(VACCINADO)

Ce te carte doit être conservée pour éviter une détention à la Quarantaine ainsi que sur les chemins de fer des Etats Unis.

Conserve-se este cartao para evitar detenção na quarantena e nos caminhos de ferro nos Estados-Unidos.

PORTUGUESE RADIO PERSONALITIES. Portuguese radio personalities pose in front of radio station KTRB. From left to right with labels are David Maciel, Celeste Santos, M. C. Liel (KGDM), A. V. Avila (KROW), J. Victorino (KTRB), S. Azevedo (KTAB), B. Mercer (KLS), Dr. J. Jackson (behind), T. Dias (KQW), and M. V. Borges. In front are T. R. McTammany (general manager, KTRB) and A. Moura (ATTY). In 1938, the most popular shows in the East Bay were *Voz do Povo* (Paul Alberquerque), broadcasting to Oakland and Berkeley; *Castelos Romanticos* (Arthur Avila), broadcasting to Oakland, *Voz de Portugal* (Thomas Dias), and *Ecos de Portugal* (Leonel Soares Azevedo), broadcasting to San Jose and Oakland. (JAF and August Vaz, *The Portuguese in California*.)

ROSE AND ALBERT CLUB, 1930S. Arthur Avila stands with the Rose and Albert Club in Oakland. The Rose and Albert Club musical group in the mid-1930s included, from left to right, the following: (first row) Lucille Bezerra, A. Costa, and Lenore Bezerra; (second row) P. Avila, A. Avila Jr., E. Santos, Albert Avila, and Marjorie Ramos; (third row) Arthur Avila, F. Lopez, director Alice Avila, M. Ramos, and Celeste Santos. (JAF.)

THE GREAT GILDERSLEEVE.
Harold Peary was born in San
Leandro in 1908. Peary was
a great singer as a child and
starting out in radio in 1925. In
1929, he got his first big break
in radio when he was cast as
Throckmorton Gildersleeve on
the *Fibber McGee and Molly Show*.
He starred in a tremendously
popular spin-off radio show called
The Great Gildersleeve, which ran
from 1941 to 1958. From 1950 to
1951, he starred as Harold Hemp
in CBS Radio's *Honest Harold,
the Homemaker*. In addition to his
recording work, he made feature
films, including four inspired
by the *Great Gildersleeve* radio
show. Peary also appeared in
more than 54 television shows,
including playing Uncle Edward
on *The Dick Van Dyke Show*
in 1963 and Mr. Goodbody
in the first episode of *The
Brady Bunch* in 1973. (JAF.)

The Great Gildersleeve: Harold Peary and comedy cast, KPO, Sunday, 8 to 8:30 p. m.

LATIN AMERICAN BROADCASTING FLOAT. Arthur Avila is pictured here in the center near the microphone. Avila was the director and owner of the Latin-American Broadcasting Company. In addition to writing for three newspapers—*O Lavrador Portugues*, *O Clarim*, and *O Portugal da California*—Avila imported Portuguese films during the late 1930s and early 1940s. He also edited the *Rose and Albert Magazine*. (JAF.)

ECOS OF PORTUGAL, KTAB. Above is KTAB, Latin-American Broadcasting Company. Below at the Oakland Auditorium in 1933 is Portuguese radio star Lionel Soares de Azevedo in a white cap in front. Soares de Azevedo and Arthur Avila had a radio war: Each vowed to raise more money than the other. Avila's show sold red tickets, and Soares de Azevedo's sold green tickets. Afterward the two went out to dinner and split the proceeds. The tickets read, "Something New in Radio Listening!!! For the best in Portuguese music from Portugal, Madeira, and the Azores as well as the latest in Brazilian music . . . For short, interesting items on the history and traditions of these lands. . .—All announced in English–Listen to the new CASTLES OF ROMANCE program and ROSINHA Monday thru Friday on KLX (910 on your dial) 3:05 to 3:45 p.m. –Send all cards and letters to: ROSINHA, CASTLES OF ROMANCE, KLX, OAKLAND, CALIF. (Write in English or Portuguese)." (JAF.)

AVILA AND FRIENDS, C. 1933. Posing in the back row are Arthur Avila (left) and his brother. In the center of the front row is Celeste Santos, Arthur's future wife. The two violas used in their show appear in the foreground. The Arthur Avila radio show was based in Oakland at KROW. Avila's *Portuguese Hour* had many loyal fans in San Leandro. (JAF.)

JORNAL PORTUGUES AND PORTUGUESE RADIO DIRECTORS. A group of women cook for a joint gathering of the *Jornal Portugues* and Portuguese radio directors. The scene is typical of the work that takes place at Portuguese fraternal celebrations, with women and men working behind the scenes to prepare food and coffee for the festivities. In the Portuguese *colonias*, it is not unusual to see the director of a fraternal organization roll up his or her sleeves to work alongside the other members of the organization. Today Portuguese residents hungry for Portuguese fusion cuisine head to Vila Cereja (Town of Cherries) Restaurant on MacArthur Street in San Leandro. (JAF.)

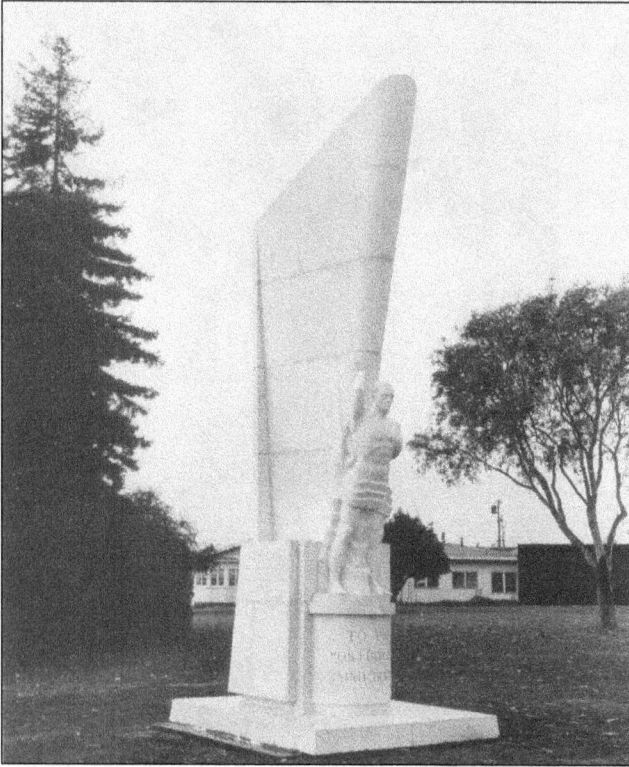

MONUMENT TO THE PORTUGUESE IMMIGRANT, ROOT PARK, SAN LEANDRO. This monument, a gift of the UPEC, commemorates the Portuguese settlers in San Leandro. The monument features the figure of an immigrant poised on the bow of a ship bound for America. On the 12-ton Portuguese marble statue is inscribed the following words from Camoes's famous poem *Lusiadas*: "And many were the countries they came from/ Leaving their homes and well-loved native Shores./ In the world's new fourth part he plows the field/ And there will go where more shall be revealed." (JAF.)

MONUMENT DEDICATION CEREMONY, 1964. Carlos Almeida, Portuguese immigrant monument coordinator, is at the podium. Next to him on the right is Harold Peary, actor and master of ceremonies of the monument's dedication held at the San Leandro Boys Club. Hal Peary was a fitting choice as master of ceremonies for the dedication of the monument honoring the contributions of Portuguese immigrants to San Leandro and the state of California. Born in San Leandro to Portuguese parents, Today Harold Peary's star shines brightly on Hollywood's walk of fame. (Carlos Almeida Collection.)

BIBLIOGRAPHY

Almeida, Carlos. *Portuguese Immigrants: The Centennial Story of the Portuguese Union of the State of California.* UPEC, 1978.

Almeida, Carlos, ed. *Centennial Souvenir Album IDES.* San Leandro, CA: IDES of Alvarado St., Inc., 1982.

Almeida, Carlos. "San Leandro Recollections," San Leandro: Historical-Centennial Committee, 1972.

California History Center. "Saga of San Leandro," Studies in Local History, Vol. 13, 1973.

Furtado, Antonio da Rosa. *Acores e o Vulcao dos Capelinhos.* New Bedford, MA: DuMont Printing, 1957.

Furtado, Antonio da Rosa. *Acores, Ilhas de Sonho.* Self-published, 1959.

Galloway, Brent. *A San Leandro Centennial Album (1772–1872–1972).* Honor Publications, A Division of Windsor Publications., Inc., 1972.

Graves, Alan Ray. *The Portuguese Californians: Immigrants in Agriculture.* Portuguese Heritage Publications of California, Inc., 2004.

Galvan, Andy. Photograph Collection. San Leandro Photograph and Document Collection. San Leandro Public Library.

Goulart, Tony P. *The Holy Ghost Festas: A Historic Perspective of the Portuguese in California.* Portuguese Heritage Publications of California, Inc., 2003.

Ilene, Herman. *San Leandro Cherry Festivals of the Past.* San Leandro: City of San Leandro, 1986.

London, Jack. *The Valley of the Moon.* New York: MacMillan Company, 1913.

Oakland Tribune. Assorted clippings prior to 1920.

Shaffer, Harry E. *A Garden Grows in Eden.* San Leandro: San Leandro Historical Centennial Committee, 1972.

Stuart, Reginal R. *San Leandro: A History.* San Leandro: First Methodist Church, 1951.

Vaz, August Mark. *The Portuguese in California.* San Francisco: The Filmer Brothers Press, 1965.

Visit us at
arcadiapublishing.com

www.ingramcontent.com/pod-product-compliance
Lightning Source LLC
Chambersburg PA
CBHW050541110426
42813CB00008B/2220